ISLAM
The True Religion

SYED QUTB SHAHEED

Translated by
RAFI AHMAD FIDAI

KITAB BHAVAN
New Delhi-2 (India)

Kitab Bhavan
Publishers, Distributors, Exporters & Importers
1784, Kalan Mahal, Darya Ganj
New Delhi-110002 (India)

Phone : (91-11) 3277392/93, 3274686
Web Site : www.kitabbhavan.com
E-mail : nasri@vsnl.com
Fax : (91-11) 3263383

ISBN : 81-7151-224-4
Code No. : I00275

First Published in India 1996
Second Edition 2001

Published in India by:
Nusrat Ali Nasri for Kitab Bhavan
1784, Kalan Mahal, Darya Ganj
New Delhi-110002 [India]

Printed in India at:
Nice Printing Press
Khureji Khas, Delhi-110051

ISLAM– THE TRUE RELIGION
CONTENTS

ISLAM — THE TRUE RELIGION

CHAPTER 1

THE NATURAL COURSE FOR HUMANITY

A Simple Fact

The truth of Islam and its practical attitude towards human life is a very simple fact, but often it is either neglected or misunderstood by the people from the outset. Consequently, a grave misunderstanding about Islam, its basic qualities, historical facts, present and future potentialities is created in their minds.

Some people, who hear that Islam is a faith revealed by Allah, assume that its behaviour to human life should be extra-ordinarily fascinating and its nature beyond the human thoughts. These people expect that Islam should neither regard human nature in practical life nor should consider the physical faculties of man. It should neither give any importance to the material aspect of human life nor should keep in view the human development and varied circumstantial changes.

People Misunderstand

Such people are despaired when they see the practical behaviour of Islam contrary to their whimsical imagination. They see that Islam does not ignore the limited human faculties and the physical facts of human life, it rather, affects them and sometimes is itself affected by them; in certain cases if it affects them then there are also circumstances when these two elements — the limited human faculties and the physical environment, are evidently in its opposite direction. And due to such effects sensuous desires, lusts, human weaknesses and faults are greatly increased and as such, man does not remain in a position to respond to the demand of the religion and follow the path directed by it. When people come across these facts, they are stunned and overtaken by despair and frustration. Their faith on the truthfulness and integrity of the religious way of life is shaken and sometimes they even become incredulous against the religion itself.

Thus, as a result of this basic misunderstanding about Islam and its system and by forgetting this simple truth, there starts a chain of misunderstandings.

Islam Is Established Through Human Efforts and Struggles

Islam is the order set by Allah Himself for human life. But it is established through the efforts and struggles of man himself. He accomplishes this living within the limits of his faculties and particular physical environment. The struggle to establish this order starts from the locus where man remains in a particular period of progress. From that very point he goes onwards on the path of Islam, according to his own toils and efforts.

One of the Basic qualities of Islam is that it neither overlooks – even for a moment – the limitations of human nature and faculties nor ever ignores the physical environment yet it carries man to such an exalted position which is beyond the approach of any man-made order. This is not a hollow pretension but a fact, witnessed by History, that by virtue of Islam man ascended to very lofty positions in the various stages of the past. And even today, if sincere efforts are made it can take the human beings to that very exaltation without depriving them of their comfort, ease, peace and tranquillity.

But as we have already mentioned above, the root of all evils is misunderstanding or ignoring the temperament of this religion and unjustly expect from it miracles which, if happen, shall alter the entire human nature. In that case neither the limitation of human capabilities nor the material realities of environment shall have any sense or importance. At this stage, however, questions may arise that if Islam is the religion revealed by Allah the Omnipotent, then why its effects and impressions are confined to the limited circle of human capabilities and faculties? Why the human faults in practical life affect it? If it is the religion of Allah then why it is not always dominating and why its followers do not gain superiority and predominance for good? Why its truthfulness and purity are covered under the clouds of physical desires and material requirements? Why human weakness prevails upon it? Why sometimes the evil forces and their adorers overwhelm the truth and its followers ?

All such objections and suspicions, as we have already stated, are raised because the reality of Islam is not properly realized but is neglected. Of course, Allah can, if He so wishes, alter the human nature through Islam or by any other means, but on account of His particular scheme He does not. He has created man with the existing human nature and favours him through His guidance according to the pursuit and solicitation of man:

'And for those who strive in us,
We surely guide them to our Paths'

(AL-QURAN, 29:69)

Allah has conferred permanent qualities upon human nature, that's why it remains constantly active. This can, neither be effaced nor suppressed from its functioning:

'And by a soul and Him Who perfected it, and inspir-

'... ed it (with conscience of) what is wrong for it and (what is) right for it, he is indeed successful who causes it to grow, and he is indeed a failure who stunts it' (AL-QURAN 91:7 10).

His Will has enforced the rule for human guidance that man can get it through the efforts and struggles he performs, living within the human limitations. This is the way also to establish the Islamic order.

'Lo! Allah changes not the condition of a folk until they (first) change that which is in their hearts.'

(AL-QURAN, 13:11)

'And if Allah had not repelled some men by others the earth would have been corrupted'.

(AL-QURAN 2:251)

Thus, Allah Himself has made it a rule that man can obtain His approbation and pleasure in proportion to the efforts and toils he exerts, the abilities and faculties he utilizes, the sufferings and pains he bears for it and the zeal he works with to wipe out evils from his individual life and surroundings.

'Do men imagine that they will be left (at ease) because they say, 'We believe and will not be tested with affliction? Lo! we tested those who were before you. Thus Allah knows those who are sincere, and knows those who are feign'.

(AL-QURAN, 29:2-3)

No Resentment or Objection

No creature of Allah has the right to resent or raise objections on the rule of guidance and instruction determined by Allah Himself and none can utter, 'Why Allah has fixed a certain way and not any others'. None can have such rights for the simple reason that a creature is after all a creature and not the Creator. A creature has neither the perfect knowledge nor the insight to guess fully the world of reasons which has its vivid reflection on every masterpiece creation of Allah. That's why the incompetent creature should not dare to utter anything against the all-comprising order of creation.

In fact, this sort of resentment or questions are raised neither in the mind of a true and sincere Muslim nor in that of a serious atheist. A true Muslim keeps away from this because the respect for Allah in his heart knows no bounds and he is well aware of the attributes and qualities of Allah. He knows well that the span of his human knowledge is quite limited and inadequate to have an apprach to the Self and Atrributes of Allah. In the same way no sedate atheist too raises such questions as he has no faith in God. If he had had faith in Allah then naturally he would know His Majestic splendour and atrributes also.

> 'We will not be questioned as to that which He does, but they will be questioned'.
>
> (AL-QURAN, 21:23)

Because, only His knowledge is perfect and only He knows the secrets of His actions.

This sort of objections and questions are, therefore, raised by those shallow people who have neither the firmness of a believer nor the constancy of an atheist. Such people are not worthy of serious consideration and there is no need to bother for them.

None, but an ignorant, who is unaware of Allah's Personality and Qualities may think in such terms. So the proper way to convince such an ignorant person is not to answer his questions promptly, but the best way is to make him understand the sense of Allah's Personality and Qualities. If he is convinced in this way and accepts the explanations, then he will enter into the fold of the believers, but if does not, then he will become an atheist and the issue will be over. This issue, however, nay take also the shape of a controversy but Islam does not permit a Muslim to be involved in such affairs.

From the above discussions we come to the conclusion that no creature of Allah has either the right to criticise the human nature created by Allah Himself, or it is befitting for any one to raise objections against the permanent and everlasting qualities of human nature. As also, nobody has the right to take exception to the system of guidance prescribed by Allah and utter, 'why the system of guidance, instead of being operative through some miraculous, mysterious and secret sources, has been left on human efforts' and is limited to the helplessness and limitations of human life.

But, in spite of this, everybody being the creature of Allah, is obliged not to ignore the facts and happenings around him. He should keep in view their reactions on human life and in this light should assess and ascertain the facts of human history, so that the historical evolution of events remains in view and he may be able to learn as well, how to face the current events and make them run towards the desired direction. Through this he will acquire the ability to lead life in the light of the Divine sagacity and nature and adopt the right attitude towards these affairs.

The last message of Allah conveyed through Holy Prophet Muhammad (S.A.W.) to the world does not take root simply because it is revealed by Allah but preachings and disseminations are also necessary for its success.

Unlike the planets and galaxy where the command of Allah is executed and obeyed quiesently by all in human life, the revealed guidance is not enforced by the word 'Kun' (Be) but here it requires a party that has complete faith in it and is in utmost harmony with it in practical life. The party should also struggle to make the guidance prevalent in the minds and lives of the people and for this purpose it should run at stake its everything. The party will have to wage a crusade against the human weaknesses and desires and against their blind followers who stand against the Truth. After passing through these stages and remaining within the human limitations and bindings of the physical environments, the standard-bearer of the truth attains success in enforcing the order of the guidance in practical life. The party, the standard-bearer of the truth, in its struggle neither overlooks the circumstances of the concerned human community nor in the various stages of the righteous path ever disregards the human needs and conditions. The party sometimes, prevails over itself and others and the rightful order is established, but there are also occasions when defeat is inflicted to the party by itself or by others. Defeat or victory, however, depends upon the efforts it makes to attain the goal and upon the accuracy of measures it takes corresponding to the situation and time. The most important of all is that how far the party-both individually and collectively, has harmonised itself with the order of the guidance.

This is the reality of Islam, its attitude towards practical life, its practical method to adorn life and the way to translate it into action. In fact this is the important factor which Allah wants to inspire into the minds of the Muslims, as declared in these verses of the Quran:

> 'Lo! Allah changes not the condition of a folk unitl they (first) change that which is in their hearts'. (13:11)

> 'And if Allah had not repelled some men by others the earth would have been corrupted'. (2 : 251)

> 'And for those who strive in us, we surely guide them to our paths' (29 : 69)

Lesson from the Battle of Uhud

And again, this very important fact was impressed on the minds of the Muslims in the battle of Uhud. In a certain stage of that battle the Muslims had descended below the standard determined by the faith and had deviated from their theory in their practical life, so Allah exposed them to a defeat. They failed to adopt the proper means and measures in consistence to the situation. They also ignored the simple fact and supposed that to be Muslim is enough to overcome in the battle. Thus Allah admonished them:

> And was it so, when a disaster smote you, though you had smitten (them with a disaster) twice (as great), that you said. How is this? Say (unto them, O Prophet); it is from yourselves.
>
> (AL-QURAN, 3:165)

He also declared

> Allah verily made good His promise unto you when you routed them by His leave, until (the moment) when your courage failed you, and you disagreed about the order and you disobeyed, after He had shown you that for which you long. Some of you desired the world, and some of you desired the Hereafter. Therefore, He made you f e from them, that He might try you'. (AL-QURAN 3:152)

The Muslim were taught this acrimonious lesson in the battle of Uhud not by means of words but they had to face the storm of catastrophe and blood and pay a very heavy cost for it. They were defeated after victory. They had to incur loss instead of war booty. They were inflicted injuries which made everyone of them restless. They had to bear the shock of the martyrdom of Hazrat Hamza, the Leader of

Martyrs and highly dignified Sahabi (Companion) of the Prophet. And above all, the Messenger of Allah (S.A.W.) was himself injured. A villainous hearted man inflicted injury on his head and one of his teeth was broken. The Prophet fell down into a pit, dug by an evil-minded ally of Abu Amir. The curel fellow had dug that for the Muslims. At that time when the infidels were attacking the Prophet, only a few devotees were left there who, one after another, sacrified their lives to save the life of the Prophet. Hazrat Abu Dujana (R.A.A.), stood in front of the Prophet like a shield. He continued to stop all the arrows of the infidels on his own back until the dispersed and aghast. Muslims were gathered there again. In this way the Muslims were taught a bitter lesson.

From this, it is quite clear that to be blessed by the guidance of Allah depends upon man's own efforts and endeavours. This manifests itself within the limited circle of human competence and thus becomes the source of purification for human soul and reformation of life. By this we do not intend to account for Allah's Will, nor we want to show the reasoning behind the order created by Him. We only want to observe and study the practical effect of His Will on the life of His slaves.

Unless a full-fledged compaign is launched amongst the people, the sincerity of faith is not proved. This compaign should end hatred and indignation from the people and bring them on the path of uprightness and Islam. The compaign may be verbal, may take the shape of propagation or may be even in the form of explanation and elucidation of Islam in reply to the unfounded objections raised against it. This may also be in the form of positive preaching. In case the obstructions are made for the people to block the road to the truth, physical strength may also be required to apply. Troubles and miseries are inevitable in this path and endurance is the necessary condition to walk on it. Even in case of victory endurance is necessary which is, perhaps more difficult than in general circumstances. After that man acquires the qualities of constancy and firmness and is capable of advancing steadily on the path of the faith.

New Horizons of Faith and Knowledge

A man cannot be exactly apprised of the reality of the faith unless he strives fully for it, among the people. For while he remains busy to strive against others, really he strives against his own self also.

As a result of such struggles, he becomes conversant with such a new horizon of faith, to which he would not have been if he would sit idle and remained inactive. By dint of these struggles he acquires such knowledge about people and facts about life which is not possible by any other means. Without passing through these paths of toils and assiduity man's soul, passions, habits and nature cannot be apprised of the altitude that can be mounted through the efforts and struggles only.

In the following words of Allah, among other things there is an indication to this fact also:

> 'And if Allah had not repelled some men by others the earth would have been corrupted'.
>
> (AL-QURAN, 2 : 251)

In the absence of these efforts and struggles, a mood of inactivity prevails on the human soul and as its first consequence there occurs the destruction of the soul which in turn causes weakness and ultimately ruination of the will-power. After that the whole life is exposed to an inertness or as it is seen in the lives of the luxurious nations, life means nothing but sensual desires.

Only Path of Prosperity

This is also an aspect of nature on which Allah has created man that he should struggle for the establishment of the religion sent by Allah. This is the only path of prosperity of human nature.

Man struggles remaining within the limited range of his capabilities and efforts. The struggles and trials to be faced in this path, reform human thoughts as well as are proved to be the sources of purification for human society. Through this the society gets rid of the idle, worthless, hypocrite, coward, deceitful and fraudulant people.

Why Troubles and Difficulties?

In fact, Allah tests the Muslims by putting them into troubles and difficulties, the sole purpose of which is that He wants to impress upon their minds the reality that they are to struggle in life. It is not possible to assess the depth of human soul without passing through the furnace, of trials, moreover, man cannot get rid of the social dirt without it. The bonfire of trials full of calamities and troubles is indispensable for the purification of the society.

When the Muslims asked why they had to face the miseries in the battle of Uhud, Allah replied:

> Say (unto them O Prophet): It is from yourselves. (AL-QURAN, 3 : 165)

He further declared

> 'That which befell you, on the day when the two armies met, was by permission of Allah, that He might know the true believers; and that He might know the hypocrites'. (AL-QURAN, 3 : 166 – 167)

> 'It is not (the purpose) of Allah to leave you in your present state till He shall separate the wicked from the good'. (AL-QURAN, 3: 179)

'If you have received a blow, the (disbelieving) people have received a blow the like thereof. These are (only) the vicissitudes which we cause to follow one after another for mankind to the end that Allah may know those who believe and may choose martyrs from among you; and Allah loves not wrong doers. And that Allah may prove those who believe, and may blight the disbelievers'. (AL-QURAN 3 : 140, 141)

In this way the Quran made it clear to the Muslims that they had to face troubles because they could not fulfil the commandments and demands of Islam in the battlefield. But it also instilled in their minds that the ultimate result was favourable for them. Allah had His kind attention again to them, He forgave their faults and made this event a lesson and source of their collective and individual rectification.

The reality of Islam and its practical behaviour towards life cannot be fully understood without taking into consideration some one or two more aspects.

The fact, that the pervasion of Islam in practice has been left on human efforts and struggles which man performs during the different stages and situations of his history remaining within his capabilities and material environment, does not mean at all, that man is quite free in this matter and there is no interference of Allah's Will and Divine Help and he may do whatever he likes. To express such a point of view in this regard is just to accept a contradiction in the Islamic conception of life.

We have already stated above, that Allah helps all those people who sincerely seek for His guidance to follow His path.

'And for those who strive in us, we surely guide them to our paths'. (AL-QURAN, 29 : 69)

'Lo! Allah changes not the condition of a folk until

> they (first) change that which is in their hearts:
> (AL-QURAN, 3:11)

These verses throw light on the reciprocal relation between human struggle and Allah's help.

With the help of Allah man attains that guidance, betterment and path of virtues for which he remains restless and longs for. From this it is evident that in this matter also, Allah's Will is the final decisive factor without which man can get nothing by himself. From this, however, only those people are benefitted who are appriseed of its action on life, long for the support of Allah and try to gain His favour.

The Divine Destiny

Man's happenings, trials, troubles and distresses all are encircled by the Divine Destiny. Nothing is out of this circle. Whatever calamity or distress befalls upon anybody or whatever success and prosperity one attains, it is according to and under the Divine Destiny.

After the battle of Uhud, Allah explaining the causes of victory and defeat to the Muslims, also apprised them of the Divine Wisdom behind it in the following words:

> 'Allah verily made good His promise unto you when you routed them by His leave, until (the moment) when your courage failed you, and you disagreed about the order and you disobeyed, after He had shown you that for which you long. Some of you desired the world and some of you desired the Hereafter. Therefore, He made you flee from them that He might try you'. (AL-QURAN, 3:152)

Through this battle, the Divine Destiny wants to show the Muslims its comprehensive path of guidance as well as signifies the active, prevailing and all-comprising Will of Allah:

If you have received a blow, the (disbelieving) people have received a blow the like thereof. These are (only) the vicissitudes which we cause to follow one another for mankind, to the end that Allah may know those who believe and may choose martyrs from among you, and Allah may prove those who believe, and may blight the disbelievers. (AL-QURAN, 3:140,141)

It means that according to the ultimate results the main factors acting behind the causes and events are the intentions and plannings of Allah which the Divine Destiny wants to execute. In this matter none can either ask for any explanation to Allah or can check Him. This is the greatest reality and fact of the faith. Unless it penetrates in the depth of man's heart, his faith cannot be perfect. As this reality of faith is very important so we have added it in this chapter for elucidation.

A Muslim, in whose core of heart there exists the natural recognition of this reality of faith, shall neither find it contradictory here nor shall he see any contradiction in the teachings of the Holy Book of Allah.

CHAPTER 2

THE SINGULAR PATH.

Why Only Islam?

Someone, may possibly ask that if, like other systems, the religion of Allah too requires human struggles and this is affected by human limitations and physical compulsions then what is the difference between this and other systems?

None of the systems is established by way of purely miracles or with the direct intervention of Allah. All systems require human struggles for their establishment. All have deep impressions of natural human limitations, normal human incapabilities, physical causes and events over them, then why all should be set aside and only this religion should be adopted, when this is also as needy as others?

To get the answers of these questions first of all it is necessary to observe the distinctive qualities of the path directed by Islam. By doing so we shall automaticaliy be aware of what is Islam in fact. The first fundamental dogma of Islam is the "Kalima-e-Shahadat". (the declaration of witness). In this we declare as witness the Unity or Oneness of Allah and the Prophethood of Muhammad (S.A.W.). By giving evidence for the Unity of Allah and His Oneness we mean that only He is attributed to the Divine essence and none of His creatures is participant in any of the Divine attributes or aspects. His first quality is His absolute authority. So only He has the right of legislation for His creatures and only He can determine the way of action for them. Only He has the right to select according to His likings, the values for their practical lives. To accept Allah as One and without any participant but not to acknowledge His right of legislation for human life and not to strive for the establishment of His system in the face of others, has no meaning. To confer anybody the right of legislation for a community or group of people means nothing else but to accept his providence, because legislation is the greatest of Allah's attributes. Similarly, to acknowledae Hazrat Muhammad (S.A.W.), as the Messenger of Allah means to accept that the path of guidance shown by him to us is the only path for the guidance of humanity. It is our duty to follow that path and make and adorn our lives according to that, so as the qualities of Islam on which we claim to have faith may manifest in our lives. This is not possible without having faith on Allah's Unity and the Prophethood of Hazrat Muhammad (S.A.W.). In other words, it means that Allah is the Master of all providence and Divine qualities and only He has the right to determine the path for human life. Man's duty is to strive fully for making his individual and collective life harmonious to the path of guidance determined by Allah and directed by Allah's Prophet Hazrat Muhammad (S.A.W.).

The distinctive eminence of this path of guidance also demands that we should try to adopt it in full.

Removes the Danger of Slavery

This is the only path that grants man the excellence, bestows on him true freedom, and saves him from the curse of slavery. Islam enables man to attain full liberty living within the circle of humanity and limits of Allah's obedience. Because, when man enters within the bondage of Allah gets freedom from the slavery of all other forces. No other order of the world has such a quality. Islam upholds only Allah as the source of all the Divine authorities and acknowledges only His right to legislate for human life. Similarly, Islam acknowledges only One God and One Lord for man. This annulls man's authority over man. No man has the right to legislate for or cammand over the others. This removes forever the danger of man's divinity and enslaving man by man.

Observing through this aspect Allah's path seems quite singular.

We do not claim this as hypothesis or presumption but it is based on facts and realities. All the prophets sent by Allah, taught the same lesson that God is One and no creature in any way, is participant or partner in His Divine Authority. A creature may have loud claims in regard to law-making for human life and these false claims may be supported by the disbelievers of God, but it does not matter. Allah says about the Christians and the Jews:

> 'They have taken as lords besides Allah their rabbis and their monks and the Messiah son of Mary, when they were bidden to worship only One God. There is no God save Him. Be He glorified from all that they ascribe as partner (unto Him)'. (AL-QURAN, 9:31)

In fact the Christians and the Jews would not worship their clergies and priests but they had made them partners of Allah in the affairs of legislation and had made over them the authority to suggest modus operandi for life. This was interpreted as worship and Allah declared that they had made their religious priests as their gods. Ascribing them as partners of Allah, they disobeyed the command that Allah the Great and Superior, is One and no one is His partner or match in His Divine attributes and authorities.

Imam Ahmad (R.A.), and Allama Ibn-e-Jareer (R.A.) have written about Hazrat Adi bin Hatim that when he was invited to accept Islam by Hazrat Muhammad (S.A.W.), he fled to Syria. At that time he was the follower of Christianity. The Muslims captured and enslaved one of his sisters and a group of his relatives. When their case came before the Prophet (S.A.W). he released the sister of Adi bin Hatim. Going back to Adi bin Hatim she narrated the events in detail and insisted him to go and appear before the Prophet (S.A.W), so he went to Medina. As he was one of the nobles of his tribe the Tai, and his father was renowned for his generosity and benevolence, so there arose a wave of pleasure and delight among the Muslims of Medina He appeared before the Prophet (S.A.W.) wearing a golden emblem of cross around his neck. At that time the Prophet (S.A.W.) was reciting this verse from the Holy Quran:

> 'They have taken as lords besides Allah their rabbis and monks.' (9 : 31)

Hearing this, Adi bin Hatim said:

"But the Christians and the Jews do not worship them!" At this the Prooeht (S.A.W.) replied, "Surely they do. Their rabbis and priests have made unlawful what Allah had determined as lawful and have made lawful what Allah had determined as unlawful. These people obey the orders of their priests which is termed as their worship."

Asadi says: "Take advice from the people but always examine it on the touchstone of Allah's Book whether it is right or wrong. As Allah says:

> "They were bidden to worship only One God."
> (AL-QURAN, 9 : 31)

From this it is evident that only the thing permitted by Allah is lawful and to commit such action which has no sanction of Allah is unlawful. Legislation from His side in any matter means that His command in that matter must be obeyed and His obedience must be observed in every case.

Islam is the religion according to which Sovereignty lies to Allah only and to direct man in regard to passing life also rests with Him. So only He is entitled to be worshipped. In this way Islam has the singular distinction of teaching man to be the slave of Allah only and it emancipates man from all other sorts of slavery. Accordingly, it is also our duty to make every possible effort to follow the path determined by Him and not to look towards any other path. As Islam is the religion sent by Allah, so there is not even a slightest reflection of human desires, weakness or selfishness in it.

This is not constituted by any individual that its ultimate goal may be the interest of any particular person, dynasty, section, nation or generation. Its Sender is Allah Himself, the Omnipotent who is the Sustainer of all. He has no selfinterest in the laws He has given to man. He has no hostility or amity with any human group. Before Him all are alike. In the laws He has given to man, no particular nation or generation is superior to any other group, nation or generation. In His eyes all are equal.

No law, enacted by any individual dynasty, section, nation or generation can be free of the desires and weaknesses of its makers. This is the weakness of human nature. So the only way to do away with this defect from human life is that Allah's law should get superiority over all.

This is also the way to introduce the complete, true and all-comprising justice. To get this sort of justice is not at all possible under any system enforced by man, because there is no human system that may be free from human desires, weaknesses and selfishness. These things must remain present in one form or other, in any man-made system. Look to these verses of the Holy Quran, what a lofty conception of justice has been introduced! This conception of justice is free from all the pollutions of human desires, passions and relations:

> 'O you who believe! Be steadfast witness for Allah in equity, and let not hatred of any people seduce you that you deal not justly. Deal justly, that is

> nearer to your piety fear Allah. Lo! Allah is informed of what you do'. (5:8).

At this stage quesiton may be asked what is the guarantee that the collective justice for which Islam commands the Muslims, shall come into force and what are the incentives that secure its enforcement in the Muslim Society?

In reply to this quesiton it may be said that the foremost and greatest guarantee for the enforcement of the Islamic Programme is the Muslims' conscience itself which grows from the seed of faith. If this faith exists in one's conscience then it is the greatest and strongest guarantee for the practical enforcement of Islam. According to the faith of a Muslim, his life, success, prosperity, conquest, power and what else he possesses, is because of his true allegiance to Islam in the absence of which declination and calamity seize him, his victories are changed into defeat and he is exposed to disgrace and distress in this world. He remembers well this mandate of Allah:

> 'Verily Allah helps one who helps Him. Lo ! Allah is Strong, Almighty. Those who, if we give them power in the land, establish Salat (worship) and Zakat (poor due) and enjoin kindness and forbid iniquity. And Allah is the sequel of events'.
>
> (AL-QURAN, 12 : 40, 41).

A Muslim is convinced that if he deviates from the commands of Allah in this life he will be deprived of His Merciful view.

The existence of Muslims Society is itself the security for the enforcement of Islamic teachings and commandments because faith is the foundation of the Islamic society and its collective responsibility is the enforcement of Allah's commadments.

In this matter even the smallest negligence and deficiency may be, in his view, a prelude to evil which he tries to avoid because it takes hold not only of bad people but the whole collective life comes within its range.

Hence, if we want a comprehensive and all-embracing order of justice in this world then to walk on the road of Islam is inevitable. We can approach our goal by adopting this singular path only.

The Second Cause

Another cause to adopt the Islamic way of life is that this is free from the defects of human ignorance and weakness. The specific defects of human nature are not found in this system. Allah, the Sender of this system is Himself the Creator of man. He knows well what is good for man. He is well aware of the delicacies and the manifold complexities of human nature. He has in view the ups and downs and states of man's life – so, He has kept all these facts in view while ordaining laws for human life. It is possible that in a certain period a man or a group of people may not see its varied aspects and they may be unable to understand its advisability as fully or partly at a time, but nothing can escape the Eyes of the Creator. To understand all these aspects fully it is necessary to have in sight all the phenomena and experiences of mankind, spread over the past the present and the future. At the sametime, the full knowledge of human life, environment and events is also necessary. Obviously, it is not possible for a human being to have the knowledge of both these factors because human wisdom and abilities are limited. Man cannot form accurate or beyond doubts opinions about the experiences he gains and the phenomena he faces. Man's nature, because of its partial and not absolute character, is deficient and imperfect. There are many lacunas in it. It is a slave of passions and a prey of weakness. So, in no way, it is fit for determining way of life for mankind. Allah proclaims:

'And if the Truth had followed their desires, Verily the heavens and the earth and whosoever is therein had been corrupted'. (AL-QURAN 23:71).

'And now have We set you (O Prophet) on a clear road of (Our) commandment; so follow it, and follow not the whims of those who know not'. (AL-QURAN, 45 : 18).

Man has not that knowledge about the reality of soul without which there can be no legislation for human life. So, whenever he goes beyond his limits and tries to propose modus operandi for life, he goes astray in the darkness of his own superstitions and ignorance, as it is not his task to frame system of life. He is even deprived of those abilities which are inevitable requirements for this. To propose a system and law for life is the responsibility of Allah and to interfere in this domain is participation with Allah which in itself is a great crime and sin.

Another Virtue of Islam

Another Virtue of Islam which demands struggles for its establishment is the system of life offered by it. It is based on a conception of life which not only clarifies the position of man in this universe but also throws light on the main goal of human life. This conception is free from the pollution of ignorance, weakness and human deception.

For the establishment of a natural system for human life, only Islam provides a solid and healthy foundation. Any system void of a comprehensive conception of life is deprived of natural support and healthy foundations. This sort of system actually is artificial and has no long life. It remains a cause of distress and troubles for humanity, as long as it exists. At last, human nature revolts against this system and it is detroyed. After this man again returns to his nature.

The conception of life granted by the Faith in Allah is the only right conception, because its source is the Creator of life Himself, who is the Creator of man and is well aware of the facts and state of life and of human nature. Except this, all other conceptions and interpretations of life are imperfect and immature. There must be one or the other defect in them. Through them neither the true conception of life can be found nor the right position of man can be ascertained. Life and man are not the synonymous words. Life is much more extensive than man, so man can neither understand it fully nor can elucidate and interpret it completely. For ascertaining the goal of human life, it is necessary to have the knowledge about the Creator and His intention acting behind the creation of man. It is also necessary to possess the ability of protection against being the prey of deception and superstition. But this is, evidently, beyond the power of man.

What are the aims and objects of human life and what is the true positon of man in this world? What the life means? Giving answers to these questions, not even two philosophers are unanimous. Some. from what the different people have said in this regard, are quite ridiculous and silly. We are amazed to see that even a philosopher can utter such silly things. But when we recall that these poor philosophers too are men as we are and they too have no source other than their wisdom in the difficult expedition for the quest of truth, our amazement is dispelled. For life and its reality cannot be contained in the narrow strait of wisdom, nor it is the sphere of wisdom. Nevertheless, when these philosophers try to answer such questions only with the help of wisdom, they actually enter into another sphere and try to go ahead with the help of wisdom as their guiding lamp. Consequently, they are stumbled again and again. Here the lamp of wisdom does not work. The world, where it works, is very limited. The real field where wisdom can be applied, is the sphere of Divine representation or vicegerency. Here man, regarding himself as the 'Khalifa' (Vicegerent) of Allah, in the light of His Orders and Commands lays the foundation of his life. From this very place man also gets the comprehensive conception of life which becomes the healthy foundation for human thoughts. With the help of this, such a natural system of life can be organized whose roots penetrate in human nature.

This is the reason that we are bound to follow the straight path of Islam in order to establish the really natural system of life. This peculiarity is not found in any other system of the world.

Concordance to the Universe

Another important reason to adopt this path is its complete concordance to the comprehensive system of the universe. As man is to live in this world so he should not adopt a system that collides with the disposition and order of this universe. And this is possible only when his planning of life is concordant to the comprehensive planning of this universe.

The harmony and reconciliation between human life and the universe is the main factor that makes human life concordant to the great forces of nature. From these forces human life gets its strength and cooperation and its energy is saved from being into collision with them. As a result of such collision man is subjected to ruination and destruction, and as such, man cannot perform the responsibility of the Divine vicegerent entrusted to him by Allah. But if his life is concordant to the Universe created by Allah, the secrets of Universe may also be discovered to him and he may exploit these secrets in his practical life. When this happens fire does not burn him but serves his purposes as his servant. He peepares his food, makes things hot and get light from it.

Basiclly, human nature happens to be fully harmonious to the temperament of the universe, so when man in his life deviates from the temperament of the universe and the principles of nature, he actually clashes with the terrible forces of nature and wages war against himself as well. Consequently, he becomes the prey of calamity, misery and restlessness. His life becomes a portrait of deprivations. As is the plight of man today, who in-spite of his scientific conquests and wild uproars of materialistic culture, is wretched and confused.

Man of Today

Man of today, as a whole is the physical structure of grief, sorrow and uneasiness. He is miserable, distressed and prey of confusion, He seeks escape from life. Sometimes he takes refuge in opium, hasheesh and wine and sometimes wishes to forget his inner anxieties through the craze of rapidity and idiotic ventures. Despite his all materialistic prosperity, plentiful productivity, pleasures, luxuries and abundance in life, man is distressed. Rather, the vacum of life and confusion are increasing as much as prosperity and abundance he is attaining. It seems as if it were a board of demons who were chasing man and he were trying to flee and evade it, but it were always taking hold of his neck.

This fact is quite vivid when we look towards the prosperous and rich nations of the world. The plight of the nations led by the U.S.A. and the U.S.S.R. is such as host of demons were running after them and they were trying to get rid of the demons as lost of themselves. Seeing them it appears that their materialistic prosperity, sensuous appetite and sexual urge going beyond the limits, have taken the shape of nerval and psychological sickness. The same is the cause of their going astray in sex, restlessness, successive sickness, insanity, abundance of crimes and lack of human respect and prestige in life.

There is no doubt that man has attained great conquests by virtue of science. He has made immense progress in the field of medicine and treatment of physical diseases. He has discovered new medicines and new methods of diagnosis and treatments. Particularly, the discovery of Penicillin and Mycine is considerable. In the same way, man has also made tremendous progress in the field of industrial products which still continues. In the conquest of space and construction of satellites and stations in space, man's success is quite evident and more success is expected. But despite all these, the question arises what man has actually got out of these struggles and progress? What effects have they produced on his life? Have they caused any spiritual growth? Has he gained the wealth of peace, comfort and satisfaction? The answer to all these questions is nothing but an emphatic 'No.' As a result of his material progress, instead of getting peace and ease, man is confronted to troubles, restlessness and fear. There is no sign of any struggle for the fulfilment of the objectives of human life. In this field man's progress is nil.

The modern conception of human life which the cultured man of today has in mind seems nothing but a curse, in comparison to that of Islam. – A curse that has thrown man from the heights of heavens to the depths of marshy land.

For instance, today in America new gods are being worshipped and regarded as the objectives of life – some of these Gods are called property some others are called 'Pleasure.' Again there are some others whom they call 'Fame'

Productivity' etc. The Americans worship these 'Gods' because they are still unaware of themselves and the main object of life is out of their sights. Same is the conditon of the other modern ignorant states. Thus we see that man has forgotten his Real Creator and is busy to worship the articicial Gods.

For thse reasons, we have no other alternative but to follow the straight path of Allah. This is the only path, following which man can return to his Real Lord and Cherisher, can acquire the knowledge about the real objective of life and current not only in human beings but also in whole universe.

The Holy Quran has made this very fact very clear and has categorically rejected the points of view of all those people who want to follow systems other than the law and system provided by Allah.

> Seek they other than the religion of Allah, when unto Him submits whosoever is in the heavens and the earth, willingly, or unwillingly, and unto Him they will be returned.
>
> (AL-QURAN, 3: 83).

CHAPTER 3

THE SIMPLE PATH

An Objection and Its Answer

It may be aaid here that the unique and great path shown by Islam cannot be practised by man for long. A human group or nation may follow this path for a short while but after that she will set it aside and follow some other path. In other paths there may not be as much elevation and greatness as in Islam but there are also not those difficulties that man faces on the path of Islam.

Outwardly, this objection appears to have considerable weight and thus many writers have tried in various ways to raise this in people's mind. They have tried to make people understand that Islam is an unrealistic and impracticable religion, it cannot be followed for more than a specific period. Islam is the standard-bearer of an idealism which is not attainable in this world. The purpose of such writers is to disappoint common man against Islam. They want to create impression in people's mind that it is not possible to bring Islam into practice. In this way they want to frustrate the efforts being made to enforce Islam in the world. These cunning critics of Islam take much interest in the disturbances after the martyrdom of Hazrat Usman (R.A.A.), in the confrontation of Hazrat Ali and Hazrat Muavia (R.A.A.) and in other such events. They repeatedly raise these topics and taking exception to such events, sometimes openly and sometimes under the disguise of critique, write and state such things which accoding to their vanity prove their devilish claims.

This sincere Muslims who read such writings become confused to think that such affairs may happen even in the golden age of Islam and may hamper its progress. Thus, they unconsciously and quite easily become tools in the hands of these cunning critics for their vile purposes. The conception of government defined to the Muslims, by the Prophet Hazrat Muhammad (S.A.W.), and his two Caliphs was clearly violated in the later period. In the same way, manners of some of the leaders of the Muslim society in that period do not come up to the Islamic standard. As the Muslims are very sensitive in such affairs, so when they see these things, begin to guess that after the short period of the Pious Caliphate all the doors of the Islamic progress were closed. The Muslims who hold such point of view, do so with their all sincerity and behind their such opinions, acts the feeling of esteem they have for the Prophet (S.A.W.) and the Pious Caliphs (R.A.A.).

The whole problem, however, deserves pondering over analysing of all the components acting behind it. For this it is necessary to understand the reality of belief (Iman), as also to know how it can guide humanity for a long time and in different environemnt and situation.

In this connection, first of all, it should be borne in mind that it is totally incorrect to state that Islam imposes such formidable restrictions on human soul which are not possible to bear for long.

Road to Islam is the greatest one and this is the only natural course. Its greatest prop and capital is the human nature. One of the virtues of Islam is that it knows well how to appeal and approach the human nature.

Islam is apprised of the natural way to approach the human soul. It also knows the formula to penetrate into the human soul, and it penetrates quite easily into it. It is also aware of the strength and capabilities of the human soul so it never goes beyond these limits. It is also conscious of the needs and requirements of the human soul which it fulfils. It has also the knowledge of the purely constructive qualities of the human soul which it avails in its positive purposes.

Despite its all greatness and elegance, Islam is basically for man and for this world, so it never overlooks the human nature or any aspect of man. It always keeps in view all the aspects.

When the human soul is coherent to its real nature, its requirements are fulfilled and its constructive qualities get the field for action then, without any compulsion, it comes into harmony with life and acquires the exaltations maintained for it by Allah. It is then, it shall not feel any difficulty passing through the long way for the noble cause. It shall rather feel it simple and plain. On that path it shall get security and self-reliance.

The people who distrust or suspect about Islam, being the practicable system, are actually afraid of its high moral principles. They fear its moral purity. They fear the responsibilities which lie on them as a result of this moral purity. They think it as an obstruction on the path of their beastly desires. They consider these bindings as a trouble and burden, so they try to avoid them. In fact, these people could not understand the genuine fact of Islamic faith. This is the main cause of their misunderstanding.

The Positive and Constructive Force

Islamic moral conduct is not the name of bindings, restrictions and prohibitory limits but in reality, it is a positive and constructive force. It is this active force that stimulates man incessantly for development and self-accomplishment. And as a result of this, the development achieved by man is second to none in its comprehensive purity. There is also a moral aspect of the positive activities and deeds performed according to Islam. Inactivity and negative attitude are immoral, for they negate the very purpose of human life. They negate the purpose attributed by Islam to Human life, which in brief is that man is the vicegerent of Allah on the earth and so it is his duty to use all the energies given to him by Allah, in constructive activities.

The growing of virtues and fight against evils is a moral issue that brightens the fundamental elements of man's personality. In the eyes of Islam, Allah's obedience is the highest moral surface and this manifests the highest moral excellence. If the moral aspects, considered to be unnecessary bindings and chains -- are analysed thoroughly, it occurs that they are actually the various manifestations of movement, liberty and strength.

As for example, the unlawful sexual activities may be taken, Islam has declared self-control for man as compulsory. It has laid great stress on keeping away from sexual anarchy. Seemingly it occurs a moral restriction, an unnecessary restraint and confinement, but this restriction, actually, emancipates man from the slavery of desires and gives excellence and strength to human intentions. This restriction enables man to have sexual satisfaction remaining within the limits of chastity determined by Allah.

Similarly there is another instance, the command for charity. This is also considered by man a burden. He thinks that because of this order he himself, neither can enjoy fully with his belongings, nor can impress others. But, actually charity enables him to overcome his greed and avarice and creates in him the feelings of collective welfare and benefits, which has broader circle than individual life. So that command about charity is not an inapt compulsion but a means of awaking the sleeping faculties of man and to bless him with the real liberty.

Here we have not enough space for further instances, yet from whatever has already been mentioned, the motive behind the moral restrictions imposed by Islam, can be easily understood.

Sins And Vices Suffocate Human Soul

Accorting to Islam sins and vices are the chains that suffocate human soul and evidently the human soul is sunk into disgrace. Thus the real freedom and emancipation in the eyes of Islam are to get rid of the sordid passions and desires. This point of view is the basis of its whole normal system.

In Islamic theory the human nature is basically good and is naturally inclined to virtues. The creation of man is on the best of nature but when he goes on the path other than that of Islam, is reduced to the lowest state:

> 'Surely, We created man of the best nature. Then we reduced him to the lowest of the low, save those who believe and do good works'.
>
> (AL-QURAN, 95 : 4–6).

From this it is obvious that the natural course of life for man is the course that is coherent to his nature. He can be free of all the chains and restrictions that have subjugated his real nature only by following this course. This is the only way of getting freedom from the slavery of desires too.

Islam wants to create the conditions and environment that can be helpful and conductive to emancipate man from the unnatural curves and evils so that his real nature may get manifestation. For this prupose it stimulates the constructive forces hidden within man. It wants to see these forces dominating on human life and to do away with all the obstructions that come on the way of human progress and manifestation of natural virtues.

Those people who consider the Islamic ethics a burden for man and think it impracticable, draw this conclusion seeing the present sorrowful plight of the Muslim Society. But the Islamic Principles have nothing to do, as they are not at work in this society. In the present society, however, it is indeed very difficult for a man to follow the Islamic ethics, as this corrupt and ingorant society has nothing to offer those people who wish to lead the life according to the doctrine of Islam except ruin and disaster.

The conception about natural circumstances before Islam is quite different from that of others. Islam is a realistic order and it expects from its followers that in their Society Islamic Law shall be dominating and active. In Islamic Society Purity and Virtues are regarded as the objective realities. Here the responsibility to defend and protect the laws rests upon the rulers of the society. There is no room for sins, vices and obscenity in this society. It is the duty of the society to suppress and efface them.

When affairs are examined through this point of view, the Islamic way of life is found very simple and easy and indeed, there seems no difficulty for individuals to follow it. Instead it becomes difficult for the individuals to resent it. To fulfil the sordid desires and commit evils are not easy in such a society. If they try to commit crimes, the active forces of society as well as their own nature stand against them. Thus it becomes very difficult to follow the path of vice in this society.

Control of Allah

For this reason Islam demands full control of Allah and his faith over the human society. It does not accept any such right for any creature of Allah or for that matter any false system created by anyone else. It rather calls any such control as sedition against Allah and to ascribe partner unto Him. As we have described earlier, according to Islam only Allah is the Possessor of the Divine Authority and only He has the right to enforce law for man. The real sense of *'La-ilaha-Illallah'* is also the same.

Islam also makes it compulsory to establish an Islamic Society, in which the Muslims shall be able to lead life according to the Faith of Allah. Islam has a fundamental difference with the man-made systems concerning life as a whole and specially the purpose of human life. In the image of man offered by the man-made systems of every age, there is no reference of Allah's Guidance. This is the fundamental difference between Islam and other systems and in this matter no understanding is possible.

For the growth of the Islamic system a particular environment with all its special values is indispensable. Indifferentism to Allah and the seditious environment do not suit it. It can grow only in accordance with the conception given by Islam and the way of life based upon it. It has its own laws for life and only the environment free from all the internal and external obstructions suits it so that neither its development is hindered nor its speed is decreased.

Only this sort of environment is the natural one for a Muslim. In this environment he can lead a life according to the Islamic doctrines with ease. In doing so he gets full cooperaton from the society and in practising Islamic ethics he gets both spiritual and social satisfaction.

In the absence of such environment life becomes impossible or at least very hard for an individual who wishes to observe Islamic Principles. Therefore, if a man wishes to lead Islamic life, can do so in a Muslim environment only, wherein Islam is an active and dominating force. If he wants to lead Islamic life in a wholly ignorant environment then it is a mistake and misapprehension.

But, if there is Islamic environment, it is quite easy to practise Islam therein. So environment is an indispensable requisite for Islamic life and this is basis of all Islamic doctrines.

This is also wrong to think that in comparison to other systems man is to face more difficulties and troubles in practising Islamic system.

The fact, on the reverse, is that on all the systems – other than Islam – that man has tested in different ages and in different countries, there are clear marks of human weakness and stupidity. This is because all these systems, fully or partly, conflict with the human nature and as a result the human soul has always incurred losses.

These systems suggest only the partly treatment and solution of human problems. They have no comprehensive solution of human problems because they cannot see all the aspects of human life. If they reform in one aspect of life, create discord and disturbance in the other aspect. Again, trying to rectify their wrong-doings they create more deformity. In this way there starts an endless chain of wrong-doings. This is the story of man-made systems untill now. This shows that man suffers much more when he practises false systems. On the contrary, it is quite easy to practice the comprehensive and all-comprising system of Islam because it is concordant to the human rature. It keeps in view all the aspects of human problems and suggests comprehsnsive solutions for all of them. This indeed reflects its all-comprehensive and all-comprising point of view.

Seeing the sufferings of human being throughout the history by false systems nobody can claim that the moral duties and responsibilities entrusted to human being by the faith of Allah is a burden heavier than that imposed on man by the false systems.

Islam looks towards the loftiest destinations yet its easiest aspect is that it neither neglects the distance of path, nor acts in unnatural haste. It does not want to go forward setting aside the intermediary positions. The road of Islam is very broad and vast. This is not limited to any individual life. Unlike the man-made systems, the traveller of this road is not worried thinking about his death before reaching his goal. The adorers of man-made systems remain constantly impatient to achieve their goals within their own span of life and ardently run towards their immediate object of efforts. Thus they disturb the natural human peace. These people cannot walk in natural and peacful pace. Their path is full of bloody revolutions. While running on that path they trample the higher human values and tread the moral standards and at last, they themselves being struck by human nature into the Jaw of destruction and annihilation. Even their artificial arms do not save them from the exemplary punishment.

The path of Islam is easy as well as pleasant. It determines for human nature a direction and path. It prevents the human nature going astray. Whenever, there appears any weakness, it gives support and strength. But it never tries to defeat or destroy the human nature. Islam, like a true and wise physician, serves with patience the purpose of human reforms. It has faith on the success of its superior and long-term object of efforts. It knows well that its object cannot be achieved through one, two, three or even a hundred or thousand steps taken in haste. The only conditon to achieve success is constant efforts by man according to the way determined by Islam.

A tree that has its top going towards the heights of the sky, first penetrates its roots in the ground. It is then that its branches and sub-branches go upward; likewise this faith too first penetrates into the human souls and gains ground. It grows and spreads gradually but with full confidence and certainty and eventually attains the position endowed by the Divine Will.

After sowing the seeds of its message in human soul, Islam takes care of it so that it should grow according to the natural pace and peace. In the whole process its main goal is neer out of sight. If, there appears any sloth in its speed or it has to retreat, it is because of human nature for which it always makes allowances. Here is an example -- sometimes plants are covered under the sands, often they are eaten by insects or are worn out and diminished; occasionally they come under floods or subjected to some other natural calamities. In all such cases the wise farmer, however, knows well that his plants will at last overcome these calamities. So he is not afraid of these things, nor he foolishly tries to make them fruitful before the due time. The case of Islam is similar to that. Softness and affection are its distinctive qualities and this is why the restrictions imposed by it are not felt at all by human soul as burden.

Here we do not want to describe the brutalities practised on human being by the man-made systems and their standard bearers. The present sufferings of human beings are just sufficient to expose them and for this reason the intelligent people everywhere in the world are protesting against them.

In the end, we want to refute the misunderstanding about Islam that it remained in force only for a very short period and then became ineffective. Some people, very cunningly and deceitfully, are out to spread this misgiving on purpose. But the fact is just the opposite -- the spiritual, social and political order evolved within one or half of a century on the basis of this great and singular system is facing successfully all sorts of inimical attacks and hostilities for more than a thousand years.

The terrible elements, with the support of all the forces of ignorance of the world, have remained incessantly active against Islam and have even infiltrated in its foundation. Yet, these forces could not eliminate Islam. As a result of the cruel concentration and constancy in actions of these forces against Islam, its strength has been weakened and the Muslims, being deviated from the fundamental principles of Islam, have reached their present plight. At the moment, although Islam has lost its strength, rather its very existence is in danger, yet no evil could infiltrate into its deep thoughts. Despite all the efforts of the enemies and antagonists the beliefs of Islam are still pure and unadulterated. From these beliefs new avenues of research may be opened and even today by adopting them a new generation may turn over the new leaf.

This is the fundamental difference between the faith of Allah and the man-made systems.

The Glorious Age.

No doubt, there was once a glorious age of this Faith, rather it was glorious for the whole of humanity. So the guidance seeking eyes still look towards this Glorious Lighthouse to get light. There is also no doubt that the span of this glorious age was too short – Yet it may be said that only this glorious age is not the whole of the Islamic history. This is the highest destination where the Divine Will wants to take man and for which it is the duty of man to struggle. As much as man will draw nearer to this destination, so much the expectation to reach there will grow in his mind. One of the aims of his struggles is to keep this candle of hope burning. So far this glorious age is concerned, it has its own position on this road of loftiness. This is the lighthouse from which the humanity gets guidance and light.

This glorious age was not the result of any supreme human miracle that it cannot be brought back now. It was, actually, the result of the human struggle of the first Muslim Society. So, if there is another ground ready to make similar efforts for that glorious age, it can be brought back and the displeased spring may come again to this garden.

The splendid struggles of that selected group are a perfect example not only for any particular generation but for the whole human race. Its manifestation through practical human life in any age depends upon the blessings of Allah and the Divine Will. If it is prominent in practical form, by seeing it, others also may get encouragement to mould their lives accordingly. Thus to bring back this glorious age depends upon the future human generation. It depends upon the extent of their struggles.

In regard to the glorious age, this should also be borne in mind that it has continuously exerted effects on the later ages and those effects have always remained prominent on the vast spheres of human life. For centuries it has exerted deep and far-reaching effects on human thoughts, history and environment. Its marks, as a whole, are prominent on the pages of history. This is the fact, indeed, that encourages us and we hope that man can attain again this glorious position if he tries again for this.

CHAPTER 4

THE PATH OF SUCCESS

With the light of Allah's faith, humanity is brightened forever. It is blessed with its brightness, elevation, greatness and all-embracing nature. The marks, it has left on human history, are perpetual. This is the reason that the present generation in comparison to past generations, save the first selected generation, has more potentialties to struggle for achieving the Islamic goal. What this generation has inherited from the past in the form of thoughts, values, ways of life and events, has considerably added to its potentialities.

Keeping in view the nature of this book, our efforts in this chapter will be to uncover some bright aspects of this distinct and shining lamp of guidance, not only from the Islamic history but also from the whole human history.

The Ideal Personalities

In the beginning of the great Islamic age the human life got some ideal human models. They represented the high class humanity. The parallel of those representatives is found neither in Pre-Islamic age nor afterwards. The personalities brought up by the systems other than Islam look like dwarfs before them, as if they were incomplete and unaccomplished personalities.

The ideal personalities brought up by Islam within a very short period are not a few who can be counted easily, rather there is a huge number of such personalities who were brought up under the inspiration of Islam. A student of history is amazed to see on one hand their greatness and firmness and on the other hand their great number. He is at loss to understand how they were brought up in such a short and limited period. There can be no other explanation but Islam for such extraordinary persons in such a great number.

We ought to know that those personalities who symbolize a superior standard of humanity and in comparison to them, all the later people look like dwarfs; and who moulded themselves according to the Islamic model, however, belonged to human class. They were neither free from human limitations nor ever suppressed their constructive potentialities. They never took loads more than their capacities. They took part, enthusiastically, in every activity of human life and enjoyed all kinds of lawful pleasures according to their cirumstances and time. They did good deeds and committed errors as well. They would stumble and stand again. Like other human beings they too had weakness. They would fight against their weaknesses and would often prevail over them.

The comprehension of this fact is quite necessary. From this, the humanity gets rays of hope for the revival of its struggles. It determines as man's right and duty to struggle for the attainment of the superior and practical object. According to it, man should always remain active to achieve this goal. This creates in man self-relience and he learns to rely on his inner nature and sleeping potentialities, which if properly utilized can help man to reach again ,the lofty destination of humanity that human history has already once experienced. Man had not reached that lofty destination as a result of an extraordinary and unbelievable miracle, but he had attained it by adopting the way of life coherent to his nature. He had attained it through his efforts and remaining within the limited human circle.

This great and exceptional generation came into

being in the desert which was poverty-stricken and naturally, economically and scientifically backward region. The sandy atmosphere was very suitbale for this kind of generation but today even in another atmosphere, if man follows the Divine guidance and goes forward on that path of life, he can reach that lofty destination again. There is no dearth of favourable inner nature and potentiality in him – he has all the required potentialities and his nature is also fully coherent to that. In the past, people deviated from the straight path of Islam and there were enmity and several hostile attacks by the antagonists yet it contunued to bring forth the ideal personalities like those of its first period. There was the bright example of the first period before all these personalities. Thus the first period has always inspired the human history through these personalities. It has changed the course of history and has left its deep marks over the world.

Even today Islam can bring forth such ideal personalities,with the only condition that by heart and soul, earnest efforts should be made to mould life according to Islam and all the obstructions and difficulties in this course should be disregarded.

The Secret of Islam's Success

The Secret of Islam's success is that it fully coheres to the essence of human nature. It has got the cooperation of human nature and can utilize fully the natural potentialities of man. Human energies and potentialities know to bounds and they are of permanent character. When they are moulded according to the intent of Islam, their immense vastness may be understood.

The ideal Islamic age of glory has granted man some principles, thoughts, values and standard of testing and examining. No parallel to them is found anywhere in history nor the vividness, depth and grasping power are seen anywhere also. Their importance for life is fundamental. No other system on earth could grant man such blessings. None of them has such vivid, deep and comprehsnsive thoughts and the instances of such truthfulness, solemnity, sincerity and uprightness are found nowhere else.

These principles, thoughts, values and standards prevail on all aspects of human life. In them there is the conception of God as well as the arguments regarding relation between man and God. There is human conception of life and also the conception of the purpose of life. There are discussions about the position of human life in the Universe as well as the issue of man's character is also dealt with. These principles, thoughts, values and standards prevail on all such problems.

So Islam through its principles and theories has produced the conception of the real human nature. It has also explained the rights, duties and responsibilities of man and has given him the scales on which his life, activities, position and rank may be measured and examined. His relations to his Lord as well as to his fellow-men are also determined on this very basis. His relations with the universe, animates and others are also indicated. All the political, social and economical rights and duties, various systems and the circumstances and relations that connect the rights and duties with each other have been dealt with in these principles and theories. In other words, the human life with its all varieties and vastness is summarised into these principles and theories.

The distinct characteristics of ideal Islamic age and distinguished heavenly seals are prominent on all of them.

But this change in the state of affairs took place in such an environment that was quite adverse to these principles, thoughts, values and standards. These thoughts flourished in a secular atmosphere where their truthfulness was suspected. They could flourish n an economic, political and social situation that clashed with the Islamic point of view at every step. It was the first chance that Islamic principles manifested on life. In short, the situation at that time was not at all favourable to the great purpose of Islamic movement. The success of Islamic movement wholly depended upon the utilization of human faculties under the Divine Guidance – The Divine Guidance that is fully cohesive to the human nature and is above the superficial impressions of time. Islam inspired and stimulated the hidden qualities of man and proved that if this straight path which makes man free from confusion and indolence, is ,adopted then there may be unlimited extension in human qualities. This straight path can also face those superficial impressions and feelings which are regarded by some short-sighted peoples as the purpose of life. But, in spite of this, Islam is neither against the impressions of time nor does neglect its influences on life. Yet it does not recognize them as irrefutable facts and so does not allow to follow them. Instead, Islam pays attention to the hidden qualities of human nature and makes them strong and powerful. It shows a path and as described in the previous chapter, it tries gently and without inflicting any torment to mould the reality in its own form. Thus the conditons of the ideal Islamic period may be brought back. The present adverse local and international situations may be changed in favour of Islam, as it was once done in Arabian Peninsula and in other regions of the world.

Present Conditon

Today the condition of humanity, in some aspect

is better than that at the time of the beginning of Islam. The change that has taken place within a short period has brought with it prosperity and satisfaction. So, now it is comparatively, easy to practise Islam than before. On this aspect we shall discuss in detail in any of the next chapters. Today man's power of endurance is much more than before. When we look at the present evils, mischiefs and destructions and see the material, economical and idealistic elements acting behind them, we are more convinced about it and our reliance on man increases. The capability of man fully awakes when he tries to proceed towards a definite direction, under the guidance of Allah's faith which is fully cohesive to the essence of human nature and the temperament of the universe. The treasure of human potentialities in its sanctity, grip and vastness is superior to all those elements that come before us in the disguise of 'Reality.' It makes, therefore, no difference if these elements look adverse today.

To those people who are unaware of the reality of Islam, the material reality is unalterable, all-powerful and no change is possible in it.

But it is a great misunderstanding and deceit. The real essence of the human nature is also a part of the 'Reality.' For the present it is not cohesive to the exterior material reality, rather it is striving everywhere against it. When human nature clashes against a particular situation or system then in the beginning it may be defeated because a certain material force acts behind that situation or system, but there is no doubt about it that the human nature is more powerful and stronger than the temporary situations and events. Particularly where it grows in accordance with a cohesive faith. Thus it is the human nature that at last overcomes.

The world has already witnessed it once when the 'active force' in the Arabian Peninsula and in the world over, clashed against the faith of Allah and in the result Allah's faith got the glorious victory over the so-called 'material reality.' It changed the whole ideal and practical foundations and laid the foundation of a new edifice of thoughts and deeds.

But this was not the result of any superhuman miracle. It was, rather, in accordance with the perpetual law determined by Allah. There was human struggle behind this, it happened through the human efforts. All the human limitations, peculiar to the human efforts, were with it.

The marks and impressions left on the life of mankind by that glorious age are in favour of a similar new struggle. These are the elements from which a new movement gets strength. This age granted mankind practical traditions and realistic insitutions based on its own principles, theories, values and standards which stood and existed even after the age had passed. Its instance is like that of a river which stretched far and wide in the world over and extended continuously to periods and ages. It influenced humanity in one way or other and ultimately became the source of strength for it. The humanity remained getting benefits from it for more than a thousand years. Its signs are visible on thoughts, events, traditions, Science, economy and, in short, on every sphere of human culture. Even today we are not free from its influences. There are tumults of hostile forces and the western world ignoring the Divine Guidance, is lost in the ignorance of Greece and Rome, yet Islam's influences exist even today as a substantial fact.

Today in the life of mankind, there are many admitted facts that have no concern with their peculiar influences, principles, values, theories and institutions, nor anybody knows their origin. Today their existence is not regarded as the effects of Allah's faith but are understood to be the result of something else. Yet, to discover their original source through their effects, to follow the path of Allah and mould the human life according to that, is not impossible. In the next chapter we shall discuss about the splendid development of humanity that has brought it nearer to that splendid road. But before fourteen hundred years, when Islam was revealed, it was bitterly opposed by the world because of ignorance.

The man of today is nearer to Islam because of his splendid developments. Today Islam is easily comprehensible for man, for he is already aware of it by virtue of his historical sense he has inherited. This facility was not available to the people in early days of Islam. Man of today has the complete history of Islam before him. Now, this fact is known to all, that whenever man went astray, leaving the straight path, he was stumbled and had to face sorrow and grief. With these facts keeping in view, it is hoped that one day mankind must embrace Islam. And this hope infuses spirit to struggle for this with endurance.

CHAPTER 5

THE TREASURY OF HUMAN NATURE

Everything Was Different

When Islam appeared, it had to face the great reality in the form of Arabian Peninsula, still more, in the form of the whole world. The beliefs, thoughts, standards and systems current in those days were all opposed to it. The situations, events, interests and loyalties too were in the opposite direction. All these forces were obstructing its path.

There was a wide gulf of seclusion between Islam and the people of Arabian Peninsula rather of the whole world. The way on which affairs of the world were going on and the powers having hegemony had further widened the differences between them. There was no common value between the new faith and them. Moreover, this new faith wanted not only to bring revolution in the beliefs, dogmas, values, standards, rituals, traditions, ethics and feelings only, but also its aim was to change the system of life, its various institutions and laws. It wanted the distribution of wealth and provisions anew. It wanted to see mankind free from oppressions, tyranny and ignorance, so that being free, they may be able to live as obedient and submissive to Allah and His faith only.

If, at that time, one would have been told that despite all these difficulties and obstructions, the new faith would prevail and would change the meanings of 'facts of life' within half a century, then one would have never believed it. One would have thought such utterrances as insanity and would have rejected it with a hateful smile.

But, in spite of that, the all-embracing 'fact' had to accept defeat before the new faith which captured the position of world leadership to bring the world in the light from the darkness, through the law of Allah.

How this could happen? At that time it seemed impossible to the people whose eyes were dazzled by the outward glitterings of the so-called 'facts'. They thought it impossible, as they could not think being above the surface of the materialistic environment around them. It was beyond their thinking that a single person Muhammad, the son of Abdullah (S.A.W.), could overcome the whole world or even in the beginning could overpower the Arabian Peninsula and could defeat the honourable leading Arabian dynasty, the Quraish and breaking the boundaries of the then current beliefs, thoughts, values, standards, adverse systems, institutions, interests and loyalties could establish quite a new system based on the new theory and belief.

No Conciliation

The Prophet (S.A.W.) did never come to an understanding or conciliation with the false beliefs and conceptions nor did ever submit before the passions and desires of those people. He never tried to make an agreement with their leadership. The Prophet (S.A.W.) never yielded to them in any matter so that he may get strength. In the beginning of his mission, when he was in Mecca, where all the inhabitants were hostile to him,,Allah gave the direction to the Prophet in the following words:

> 'Say: O disbelievers ! I worship not that which you worship; nor worship you that which I worship. And I shall not worship that which you worship nor will you worship that which I worship. Unto you your religion, and unto me my religion'. (109 : 1 – 6)

He did not think it sufficient, only to declare the religious differences between himself and his opponents nor he thought it enough to declare the different way of prayer and the unfathomable gulf of differences, but also, according to the dictun of Allah, he declared in clear terms that in future too, there was no hope of accord with them. He declared once more:

'And I shall not worship that which you worship, nor will you worship that which I worship'.

He was ordered to declare in clear terms the existence of the unfathomable gulf between him and the infidels, as:

'Unto you your religion and unto me my religion'.

But, throughout all these stages, the Prophet neither ever claimed to have some mysterious forces in his possession, to make the people awe-struck, nor he ever demanded any superhuman preferences. He was directed to state:

'Say (to the disbelievers): I say not unto you (that) I possess the treasures of Allah, nor that I have the knowledge of the unseen; and I say not unto you that I am an angel. I follow only what which inspired in me.' (AL-QURAN, 6 : 50)

He never tried to attract people to become his followers by enticing them for high ranks and wealth. Ibn-e-Ishaque writes:

"During the days of Hajj the Prophet (S.A.W.) would go to various tribes and would say, "O, people of such and such tribe, Allah has sent me unto you as his Messenger and has commanded you to worship only Him and should not make anyone His partner. So give up worshipping those idols whom you have remained worshipping till now. Have faith on my prophethood and help me to fulfil the responsibilities that Allah has entrusted to me."

It is also related by Ibn-e-Ishaque, as narrated to him by Al-Zahri that one day the Holy Prophet (SAW) called on Bani Aamir bin S's S'ah and gave the message to worship only Allah the Al-mighty. Hearing this Baijrah-bin-Faras, one of the members of the tribe expressed, "By God, if this fellow of the Quraish becomes a companion of mine, I can overcome the whole of Arabia." Then addressing the Prophet (S.A.W.) he asked:

"If we acknowledge allegience to you and tomorrow, by the Grace of Allah, you overpower your enemies, then shall we get power after you?" – "Allah is the Possessor of power," replied the Prophet (S.A.W.), "and He grants it to whom He likes." Hearing this the man said, "Do you mean to say that we should declare war against the whole of Arabia but when Allah helps you and you prevail upon them yet we shall not get power? We do not want your such religion." And thus, they did not agree with the Prophet (S.A.W.).

Now, the question arises, how such a great revolution could take place, and how a single person could change the overwhelming 'reality' around him?

The Material Fact Was Defeated

In order to overcome the 'material facts' around him, the holy Prophet (S.A.W.) did not get any support from any extra-ordinary miracle. He totally refused to show such miracles and attract people through them. He never gave any importance to miracles. Whatever he did was in accordance with the common natural laws and anybody could practise that.

The fundamental cause of success of Islam was that it had attained the full-fledged cooperation of the human nature which was hidden behined the outwardly 'facts.' The human nature was fully cohesive to it. As we have stated earlier, the faculties of human nature have infinite vastness. When they are evolved on a particular way and are centred on a certain point, then no superficial and external obstruction can stand against them.

At the time when Islam was revealed, man was enslaved by the false and untrue beliefs and theories. The House of K'aba and man's heart and mind were under the subjugation of the false gods. Tribal and economical interest moved around those false gods. Behind them were hosts of the attendants of the House of K'aba, the atrologers and the priests who stood as the protectors of the false gods. This situation was created because of making human beings partners in the divine qualities and entrusting to the astrologers and priests the authority to legislate for man.

To change the situation, Islam presented the conception of the Unity of God. It approached directly the human nature which basically accepts only One True God. Islam made man aware of the Real Lord and of His atrributes and excellence. By nature, everyone has this sense but at that time it was covered under the rubbish of the false beliefs and theories.

> "Say: Shall I choose for a protecting friend other than Allah, the Originator of the heavens and the earth, Who feeds and is never fed? Say: I am ordered to be the first to surrender (unto Him). And be not thou (O Muhammad) of the idolaters.
>
> Say: I fear, if I rebel against my Lord, the retribution of an Awful Day.
>
> He from whom (such retribution) is averted on that day, (Allah) has in truth had mercy on him. That will be the signal triumph.
>
> If Allah touches you with affliction, there is none

that can relieve therefrom save Him, and if He touches you with good fortune, there is none that can impair it; for He is able to do all things.
He is the Omnipotent over His slaves, and He is the Wise, the Knower.
Say: (O Muhammad): What thing is of most weight in testimony? Say: Allah is witness between you and me. And the Qur'an has been inspired on me, that I may warn herewith you and whomsoever it may reach. Do you in sooth bear witness that there are gods beside Allah? Say: I bear no such witness. Say: He is only One God. Lo ! I am innocent of that which you associate (with Him)."

(AL-QURAN, 6: 14-19)

"Say. I am forbidden to worship those on whom you call instead of Allah. Say: I will not follow your desires, for then I should not be of the rightly guided. Say: I am (relying) on clear proof from my Lord, while you deny Him. I have not that for which you are impatient. The decision is for Allah only. He tells the truth and He is the best of Deciders.
Say: If I had that for which you are impatient, then would the case (ere this) have been decided between me and you. Allah is best aware of the wrong doers. And with Him are the Keys of the invisible. None but He knows them. And He knows what is in the land and the sea. Not a leaf falls but He knows it, not a grain amid the darkness of the earth, naught of wet or dry but (it is noted) is a clear record.
He it is Who gathers you at night and knows that which you commit by day, then He raises you again to life therein that the term appointed (for you)

> may be accomplished. And afterward unto Him is your return. Then He will proclaim unto you what you used to do.
> He is the Omnipotent over His slaves. He sends guardians over you until, when death comes unto one of you, Our messengers (i.e. angels) receive him and they neglect not.
> Then are they restored unto Allah, their Lord, the Just. Surely His is the Judgement. And he is the most swift of reckoners.
> Say: Who delivers you from the darkness of the land and the sea? You call upon Him humbly and in secret, (saying): If we are delivered from this (fear) we truly will be of the thankful. Say: Allah delivers you from this and from all afflictions, yet you attribute partners unto Him. Say: He is able to send punishment upon you from above you or from beneath your feet, or to bewilder you with dissension and make you taste the tyranny one of another. See how We display the relevations so that they may understand."
> (AL-QURAN 6: 56 – 65)

In this vast and extensive desert of misbeliefs, the human nature heard this call from within the thick curtains of the so-called 'facts' and returned to its Real Lord. Thus the new call prevailed upon the material fact.

After having faith in Allah, it became impossible for man to worship another man. When all heads bowed before One Allah, the Omnipotent, all became exalted and then all prides of race, dynasty and nobility and all distinctions of ruling and monarchy were abolished.

But, how this event could take place?

In the Arabian Peninsula

Elements of class, race and materialistic thoughts were active to back up the prevailing social 'facts' in the Arabian Peninsula and in the world over. This was the 'admitted fact' of the day and it was quite impossible to raise voice against it. The vested interests were naturally silent and those who were crushed by it were just unable to protest against it.

The Quraish had determined themselves as the nobles and so they were entitled to such legacies and rights which other Arabs were deprived of. Of example, during the days of Hajj all were to assemble in the plain of Arafat, save the Quraish who would stay at the 'Muzdalfa'. Because of these preferential rights, the Quraish had attained economical superiority to other Arabs. Anybody intending to observe 'Tawaf' (circumambulate) around the house of K'aba, was compelled to buy cloth for it from the Quraish and perform Tawaf wearing these cloth. Otherwise, he would have to perform Tawaf without any cloth.

At that time, the racial superiority and distinctions prevailed also in the world around the Arabian Peninsula.

The Iranian Society

The foundation of the Iranian society was laid on the distinctions of race and profession. There existed an unfathomable gulf of differences between the various classes of society. For a common man it was prohibited by the state to purchase the property of a rich man or prince. An important feature of the Sasanid Society was the compulsion that everybody should accept his family positon and nobody should amend to go beyond that. None should have even a longing for the work or occupation other than that god had destined for him. The Iranian monarchs never considered common man worthy to get a share in power. The common people too were divided vividly into different classes and every class had its particular positon.

The Iranian rings claimed that they had the blood of gods in their veins. So the common people would regard the Kings as gods. They thought that the kings possessed super-human divine characteristics. Thus they would pray to them for the remission of their sins, would acclaim their divinity and thought them above the law, criticism, human weaknesses and every kind of fault. To address the king by name or to sit near him was considered a disrespect for the king. People were bound to obey the kings but the kings had no responsibility in regard to their subjects. If they ever granted even a meagre portion of their countless wealth, it was considered as their mercy, otherwise the poor people had no legal right to get any benefit from the royal treasury. The people were considered as to submit before the king and obey him. The Kayani dynasty considered it as its article of faith that no dynasty or individual, save the Kayani dynasty, had the right to rule over the people and receive taxes from them. The king's son would inherit this privilege from his father and nobody could dare to utter even a single word of criticism against it. He, whoever dared, was treated as a rebel and tyrant. The hereditary monarchy and inherited authority of the royal family was an admitted fact which required no alternative system. In the absence of a major male member in the royal family, a minor child of the royal family would ascend the throne and full authority would be entrusted to him. If there would not be a minor male member, even a woman of the royal family would become ruler. For instance, when after Shirve his son Ardashir ascended the throne, he was a child of only seven years. In the same way, Farrukhzad a Khusraw, the son of Khusraw Perviz ascended the throne in his childhood. Buran, the daughter of Kisra (Khusraw) and Azrami

Dukht too were enthroned on the same principle. While doing so, none could think that there were famous generals and leaders like Rustam and Jaban, who deserved the position more than the women. It was not considered because they did not belong to the royal family.[1]

In India

In the same way, caste system in India was the worst type of man's tyranny over man.

Three centuries before Jesus Christ, the Brahmin culture flourished in India which influenced the Indian society deeply. A new civil and political code was formed. This code named as "Manu-Shastra" had religious support.

The code divided the nation into four distinct classes. The first class consisted of the Brahmins, priests and other religious people. The second one consisted of the "Khashtries" or the warriors. The third class was composed of the "Vaish" or the farmers and traders. The fourth class was called as the "Shudras" and its function was to serve all the other classes.

Manu, the legislator of the said code states:

"For the benefit of the world, the Omnipotent created the Brahmins from His mouth, the Khashtries from His arms, the Vaish from His thigh and the Shudras from His feet – and for the welfare of the world He has entrusted different duties and responsibilities to them. The Brahmins are entrusted with imparting the knowledge of the Vedas to the people, offering sacrifices to the deities and receiving alms and

---

1. See the book "What Harms got the world by the Decline of the Muslims", by Maulana Abul Hasan Nadvi.

charity. The Khashtries are to defend the people, offer sacrifices, study the vedas and to avoid running after the desires. The functions of the Vaish are cattle-farming, to study the Vedas and the performance of trade and agriculture. The Shudras are to serve the above three classes.

"Granting special privileges to the Brahmins this code made them akin to the deities and ascribed them the position of the chosen ones and the best of creatures. Whatever exists in the world, belongs to them. They are the rulers and the rest of the world is their subject. They can snatch away anything they like from their slaves, the Shudras. This is not a crime, because whatever they possess actually belongs to their Brahmin Masters. No slave can claim for anything as his own, whatever he has is actually of his master. All the sins of a Brahmin, who commits to memory the Rigveda, are automatically pardoned even though he destroys the whole world. The King has no authority even at the most critical juncture to receive any tax or tribute from a Brahmin. No Brahmin, although liable to death sentence should be exposed to death with hunger and fast."

Although the position of the Khashtries is superior to that of the Vaish and Shudras yet they are inferior to the Brahmins. Manu writes:

"A ten-year-old Brahmin is superior to a hundred-year-old Khashtri just as a father is superior to his on.

So far the untouchable Shudras are concerned, according to this religious and civil code, their position is worse than the animals rather worse than the dogs. Manu's law states: The happiness and pleasure of a shudra depends upon his service to the Brahmins. Save this, he is not entitled to get any prize or remuneration. The Shudras are not allowed to earn money or accumulate wealth because it annoys the Brahmins. If a Shudra attacks upon a Brahmin with his hand or club, his that hand should be chopped off. If he kicks a Brahmin, being enraged, his that foot should be chopped off. And if a Shudra tries to sit in the association of the Brahmins, the King should either mark his buttocks with fire, or should exile him from the kingdom. In case a Shudra abuses a Brahmin, his tongue should be cut out and if he poses himself as the friend of a Brahmin, he should be made to drink boiled oil. The blood money of a Shudra is equal to that of a dog, cat, frog, lizard, crow or an owl.[1]

The Roman Culture

The structure of the famous Roman culture was also based on the luxuries provided by the slaves (consisting three-fourth of the population) for the nobles and aristocrats (consisting one-fourth of the population). There was vivid distinction in the law between the slaves and the masters and between the nobles and commoners as it was written in the famous statute of Justinine:

> "If anybody commits a sexual crime against a lady, widow or virgin, half of his wealth should be confiscated as punishment in case he comes of a respectable family, but if he belongs to an inferior family he should be flogged and exiled from the country."[2]

Islam Addressed the Human Nature

This was the state of affairs in the world when Islam addressed directly the human nature which was already disgusted at the situation. Thus the call of Islam changed the whole situation. The human nature heard that, addressing the whole of human world, Allah, the Omnipotent says:

---

1. Ibid Abul Hasan Ali.
2. Ibid.

> " O mankind ! Lo ! We have created you from a male and a female, and have made you nations and tribes that you may know one another. Lo! the noblest of you, in the sight of Allah, is the best in conduct. Lo ! Allah is knower, Aware."
>
> (AL-QURAN, 49 : 13)

Addressing the Quraish especially, He ordered them :—

> "Then hasten onward from the place whence the multitude hastens onward, and ask forgiveness of Allah." (AL-QURAN, 2: 199)

The Prophet of Islam (S.A.W.) addressing the entire humanity said:

> "O people ! Your Lord is One. You are offsprings of one father. You are all children of Adam and Adam was created from the soil. In the sight of Allah, the noblest is more God-fearing. No Arab is superior to a non-Arab, no non-Arab to an Arab, a black to a white or a white to a black, except by virtues and fear of Allah."

The Prophet addressing the Quraish especially declared:

> " O pepple of Quraish ! save your souls by spending money in the path of Allah because nothing will help you before Allah. O sons of Abd-e-Manaf ! nothing will be helpful for you before Allah. O Abbas, the son of Abdul Muttalib ! nothing will be useful for you before Allah. O Fatemah, the daughter of Muhammad (S.A.W.)! take from my wealth whatever you like but nothing will help you before Allah."

The human nature listened to this call and according to the immortal law of Allah, the great revolution took place, whose marks are prominently affixed on the pages of history and which may re-happen anywhere if the Divine laws are followed.

The Usury System

In the Arabian Peninsula, the business based on usury was common. The whole economic structure of the country stood upon usury. Here, nobody should misunderstand that the unsury business was limited to the individuals only, but the Quraish would do this business on a wide scale in Syria during the summer and in Yeman during the winter and their large capital was invested in this business. At the time of the battle of Badr, the caravan which the Muslims had wanted to stop on the way and for which Allah granted them a good substitute, included one thousand camels loaded with the merchandise of such business. If the usury business would have been limited to individuals only and would not have been current as a universal economic system, the Quran would not have mentioned it repeatedly, nor it would have condemned it so frequently. The Hadees (tradition of the Holy Prophet) too would not have declared it emphatically unlawful.

The fact is that the whole capital in trade, all the commercial activities and the foundation of the whole Arab economy was established on usury. The experts of economics of different countries had already agreed on the system of interest much before the prophethood of Hazrat Muhammad (S.A.W.). The economy of all the countries was based on usury. The same was the position in Medina where the Jews dominated the economy. And it is obvious that the Jewish economic system fully stands on usury. This was the 'economical fact' that administered the then Arabian life.

Economic System of Islam

When Islam came, it rejected this oppressive and criminal system and granted the world a new economic order in the form of Zakat (poor due). Qard-e-Hasanah (interest-free loan) and mutual cooperation and support :–

> "Those who spend their wealth by night and day, secretly and openly, verily their reward is with their Lord, and there shall no fear come upon them neither shall they grieve. Those who swallow usury cannot rise up save as he arises whom the devil has prostrated by (his) touch. That is because they say: Trade is just like usury: whereas Allah permits trading and forbids usury. He unto whom an admonition from his Lord comes, and (he) refrains (in obedience thereto), he shall keep (the profits of) that which is past, and his affair (henceforth) is with Allah. As for him who returns (to usury) – such are rightful owners of the Fire. They will abide therein forever. Allah has blighted usury and made alms-giving fruitful. Allah loves not the impious and guilty.
> Lo ! Those who believe and do good works and establish prayer and pay the poor due, their reward is with their Lord and there shall no fear come upon them neither shall they grieve.– O you who believe ! Observe your duty to Allah, and give up what remains (due to you) from usury, if you are (in truth) believers. And if you do not, then be warned of war (against you) from Allah and His Messenger. And if you repent, then you have your principal (without interest). Wrong not, and you shall not be wronged. And if the debtor is in straitened circumstances, then (let there be) posponement to (the time of)

ease; and that you remit the debt as alms-giving would be better for you if you did but know.
And guard yourselves against a day in which you will be brought back to Allah. Then every soul will be paid in full that which it has earned, and they will not be wronged." (AL-QURAN, 2: 274-281)

The Human Nature Responded

Hearing this teaching, the human nature cried out that the thing towards which the faith of Allah invites them was far better than its prevailing condition. When it became disgusted with the hateful prevalent system based on ususry, it changed the "misleading fact"in spite of various economical difficulties. And thus, it was proved once again that the human nature is competent to overcome all the material obstructions. The Muslim Society was purified of all the dirts of the days of ignorance, it got a new life and purity from it. Once again, it was manifested that how much dominance the false beliefs may have, but whenever the human nature is called towards the path of guidance, it certainly pays attention to it. This Is the Divine Law in This Connection.

In this regard we shall be content to present three instances of the victory of human nature over the material facts and shall demonstrate that it could survive the invasions of the false beliefs and succeeded to overcome, the illusive fact based on apathy and ignorance, by virtue of Divine Guidance. The then prevalent beliefs, thoughts, events traditions and economic factors were called as "facts." He, who is unaware of the faith and belief on Allah and of the unlimited powers of the human nature, thinks these factors as invincible and thinks it useless to oppose them. But it is not so. These factors cannot stand before the faith on Allah and human nature.

Islam never surrendered before these ostensible 'facts." It has always tried successfully to remove or change them and has established, in place of them, its own distinguished and superior system having a strong and deep foundation.

The event once already happened may happen again. What already happened earlier was not the result of any extraordinary miracle, but it was the result of the continuous process of the law of nature. The system established by Islam was based on the capability of human nature which can be used by everyone. One can make it a source to accumulate his strength, can divert it towards a particular direction and put it on the right path.

Man of today has much more ability, than his predecessors, to walk on this path because there still exist, the footsteps of the caravan of Islam to lead him. This caravan had to face the most bitter opposition but that could not deviate it from its path. The caravan continued to advance on its path and left behind it such bright footsteps that are unparalleled on the road of human history.

CHAPTER 6

THE EVIDENCE OF EXPERIENCE

When the humanity first heard the call of Islām, it was only the human nature that came to support it in the face of adverse situation. The human nature was in favour of Islam. Although the layers of destruction, human ignorance and indiference to the Divine Guidance for centuries had covered it, yet it gave encouraging response to the call of Islam and thus cleared off the rubbish amassing for centuries.

The Period of Elevation

This was a very prominent period. It was a period of magnificent elevation, a period of exceptional generation. It was a high and lofty lighthouse. It was, as we have already stated, the decision of Allah, the decree of His Will that this eminent ideology of life should take substantial and perceptible form in real life. This ideal life should be kept as a model, in the ages to come, so that it should be manifested again and again within the circle of human limitations and abilities.

It was not the natural outcome of the environment but it was the moulding of human nature into substantial facts. The way before it was clear, leadership and guidance was available and the necessary movement to stimulate and advance was also present.

Why the Elevation Could Not Be Retained?

But the humanity still, was not able to retain for long

that elevation of greatness which the selected human generation had attained. There is no other instance in history of the high speed Islam spread with. As a result, large groups of people entered into the fold of Islam. These groups were so large that no deep, unique and gradual system for their teachings and trainings could be managed. Thus, the influences of the false beliefs and ideas of the days of ignorance which the common people entering in the fold of Islam had brought with them, could not be fully evaded. Ultimately, the society once again fell down from those elevations. Now for humanity a very high jump is required to ascend again on that elevation where the selected generation of the world had reached. That generation had been prepared through unique, distinguished, deep and gradual training, It granted brilliance to the capabilities of human nature and the humanity got the right path towards evolution.

Although the Muslim society could not maintain the height it had ascended to, for more than a thousand years, yet no other society of the world could reach, even now, those elevations which the Muslim society had introduced to the world. Rather, as a matter of fact, the other societies received light and warmth in this matter from the Islamic society, the History testifies it.

Its Effects Still Exist

The splendid and unique progress made by humanity, under the influence of Islam and the elevations on which it remained for about one thousand years, cannot be regarded as merely of no avail and their effects no longer exist. and the human world cannot be benefitted from it now. It was their influence that brought a great revolution in the affairs of the world and totally changed the face of the world.

In regard to life and humanity the law of Allah is

different. Humanity is the name of a compact unity that encircles extensive lengths of time. This is the basic system that utilises the past experiences and various means and resources of knowledge. These means and resources of knowledge, at that time, were covered under the darkness of ignorance and man was going astray because of his inwardly blindness. But, in spite of this, the resources always existed. Their relation to the body of humanity is similar to that of the blood running in the veins of man.

In the beginning, Islam gained only the favour and support of human nature by dint of which it totally changed the conditon of human life. (We do not describe here the scanty moral force that existed in the world at that time as a result of the earlier religions, which unlike Islam, were not universal but limited to some particular nations only.) But today, Islam has not only the support of human nature but also the backing of the means and resources left by the first period of Islam. Today we have before us the bright examples of the people who had faith in Islam and of those who enjoyed life under the Islamic regime and were impressed by it. Similarly, Islam gives salvation to man from the bitter consequences that he had to experience because of his negligence and apathy towards God.

In the beginning when Islam had only the support of human nature, it rejected all the principles, ideas, values, measures, systems and institutions of the age, and then in a particular period, it established its own principles, ideas, values, measures, systems and institutions in the life of a group of people. Then came another period when these were established in the world of Islam and thus the whole world became aware of them. This condition persisted for about thirteen hundred years. During this period, if the institutions and principles of Islam were not present in practice and experiments, yet they were known in the world of thoughts as an ideology and as a hope for future.

Thus, when they were expressed, the humanity did not feel them strange as it had felt them in the beginning of Islam, and there seemed no aversion between the passions and traditions which existed before Islam. It is correct that the humanity, as a whole, did not show the deep perception and sagacity in regard to Islamic teachings, a glimpse of which was seen in the lives of the first selected group of Muslims in their unparalleled period.

Today Man is More Capable to Accept it

This is also correct that when in the past and in the modern age man wanted to apply some of the Islamic principles on the changed conditions then he could neither comprehend their spirit nor could succeed to apply them on his conditions. Similarly, this is also correct that now when the humanity wants to step forward, towards the goal shown by Islam, it stumbles at every step – and thus fails to approach it, though the Muslims of the first period had got it just in one jump. But despite all these things, today the humanity as a whole, is ideally more competent to walk on the inspired road of Islam and today it is nearer to Islam than before. As much it was difficult to walk on that path in the past, so much it is easy today to walk on.

Without going into details, we shall try to make understand this point through some instances, for two reasons: First, this is only a part of the vast topic 'The Faith of Islam'. To me a permanent and detailed discussion is not possible here. Second, the first wave of Islam has influenced the whole of human life and every part of the earth. These effects are so extensive in every direction that no single writer can fully circumscribe them, even though he wants to. Long ago, these influences of Islam inspired the entire world of humanity in such a way that now they are absorbed in human life. Moreover, their circle is so extensive that an onlooker cannot feel them at a glance.

Briefly, we can also describe it that the all-embracing Islam has not ignored even a single aspect of human life. In different aspects its effects may be a bit more or less, but there cannot be two opinions about their existence. It has impressed every aspect of life. All the great historical events were, directly or indirectly, the echoes of this magnificent event.

May it be the Religious reformation movement of Luther and Kelvin or the Renaissance movement of Europe, from which it is still impressed, may it be the abolition of Feudal system, or the movement of man's freedom from the capitalists' regime, may it be movement of socialism or the struggles for human rights, resulting as England's Magna Carata and the French Revolution; generally all these are regarded as the magnificent historical events, and fundamentally they are all the products of Islamic influence. All of them have clear effects of Islam on them. Dr. Ahmad Amin in his Arabic book, "Duhal Islam" (the Rise of Islam) writes:

> "Among the Christians, there arose such movements that had vivid impressions of Islam over them. The movement that arose in Septamania [1] in the eight century of the Christian era (second century (Hijra)) was one of such movements. The standard-bearers of this movement were against "Confession" before the

1. Septamania is an ancient county (district) in France and is situated on the South-West of the Mediterranean Sea.

clergymen. They would say that man should approach only God for the forgiveness of his sins. In Islam there are neither the clergies and monks nor Rabbis. It does not favour any such confession. Similarly, there arose another movement called 'The Iconoclasts'. Its object was to destroy the religious partraits and idols. During the eighth and ninth centuries A.D., (third and fourth centuries of the Hijra era) among the Christians, there emerged a sect which rejected the sanctity of religious portraits and idols. The Roman King Leo III, in 726, A.D. through a decree banned the worship of portraits and idols. In 730 A.D., through another decree, he declared their worship as idol worship. In the same way Constantine V and Leo IV also opposed idolatory. On the contrary the Popes of Rome, Gregory II and III, as also Germanus, the great priest of Constantinople supported idolatary. The Queen Irene too was its supporter. A serious confrontation raged between these two sects of the Christians, but it is not possible here to narrate it in detail. Here we want to describe only the fact that some of the historians determined the movements against idols and portraits as the consequence of Islamic influences. Thus it is said that Claudius, the Bishop of Toren (who was appointed as Bishop in 828 A.D. or 213 of the Hijra era), set on fire portraits and crosses and prohibited their worship within his domain, as he was born and brought up in the Islamic city of Aundalusia.

Simillarly there was another Christian sect that rejected the Trinity therory with the reference of God's Unity. These people also denied the divinity of Jesus Christ."

In the eleventh century A.D. when the savage armies of the Christians returned to Europe from the Islamic world, the superior pattern of the Muslim Social life was still fresh in their minds. The Muslim world, in spite of its all deteriorations was still evidently superior to the Christian Europe, for there was the rule of law and it was equally operative both for the common man and the rulers. Unlike Europe, the Islamic law was not the product of the personal will of an absolute king or of the wishes of the feudal vassals. The individuals were at full liberty to choose occupation for them. They had the right to have personal property and free trade. The society was free of any hereditary cast system anybody could obtain the highest rank in the society by virtue of his labour and ability. These things were quite new for a man of feudal Europe. He was confined to his own land and had no free status. The will of his master was law for him. He would get only the status and class as the heritage from his forefathers. He would not change his hereditary rank and position in the society, even though he wanted to.

Thus the economic elements active in the European society created the indignation that gradually abolished the feudal system and individuals attained liberty from the slavery of landlords; yet these currents of indignation could not set free man from the other bondages or slavery nor could raise the European society as high as the Muslim society.

Under the influences of the Islamic universities of Muslim Spain and the Oriental Islamic culture-which was an international culture-there arose the European Renaissance movement in the Fourteenth century and afterwards. This got strength from the Islamic sciences and arts, translated into European languages. In this way the new scientific movement flourished and subsequently the method of research was found.

Mr. Brifeld, in his book 'The Making of Humanity' writes:

"For the new world the most important present from the Arab[1] culture was the knowledge of Science, although, in producing fruits, its speed was slow. When the sagacity, created by the Arab culture in Spain, began to show its effects, several centuries had already alapsed of this culture being abolished and buried under the dark pages of the past. It was not only Science that created new life in Europe, but some other effects of the Islamic culture too were active in this regard. Although, no aspect of the European advancement is free from the obligation of the Islamic culture yet the domain, in which the effects of Islamic culture are most prominent and vivid, is the ability that bestowed it the distinct and durable force. By this we mean the scientific knowledge and the spirit active in scientific research."

The writer further writes

"Our science is grateful to the Arab science not only because it has enriched it rhrough its wonderful discoveries and new theories, but also, for the reason which is the main and more important – is that its very existence is obliged to it. As we have already seen, there was no existence of science in the ancient world. The Greeks would regard Astronomy and

---

1. Note, how the Western writers use the term of 'Arab culture' instead of 'Islamic culture'. This is not incidental but it shows that they can't tolerate even the name of Islam, so they want to confine Islam to the Arabs only. The circle of Islam, however, is far more vast than this. The real object of these gentlemen is to spread racial prejudice in Islamic Society.

Mathematics as foreign science, imported from foreign countries and adopted from foreigners. Although these learnings had become part and parcel of the Greek culture yet the Greeks never thought them as their own. The Greeks regularized the laws of these learnings and offered new theories about them but so far the intellectual scientific research, collections of positive materials, precise and continous observation and experimental methods of research are concerned, they always remained as foreign for the Greek mind. In Europe, the appearance of the knowledge, which we today call as 'Science' is obliged to the awakening of the new spirit of research, experimental and observational methods of research and the unparalleled advancement of Mathematies, which the Greeks had not even imagined ... It were the Arabs who introduced this new spirit and methods of research into the European World."

This writer, on another occasion writes :

"Roger Bacon learnt Arabic language and Arab Science in Oxford from the pupils of the Arab scientists of Muslim Spain. The credit for inventing the experimental method goes neither to Roger Bacon nor Francis Bacon, having the same nickname, has no share into this. In Christian Europe, Roger Bacon has no better position than that of a messenger of the Muslim Science and method of research. "In his opinion the only way to acquire real knowledge was to study Arabic language and Arabic learnings. So he always drew the attention of his ontemporaries towards this. How the facts about the origins of the European culture have been mutilated, the discussions concerning the experimental method

> are one of the instances of such mutilations. It is a fact that in the time of Bacon the research method of Arabs had become current in a very great part of the world and people everywhere in Europe were impatient to learn it.
>
> 'From where Roger Bacon acquired the informations regarding the scientific knowledge? From the Islamic cities of Aundalusia; so much as the fifth chapter of his book 'Cepusmajus', in which he has dealt with 'opthelmics' is the complete rendering of Ibn-al-Hitham's book "AL MANAZIR".

Professor Dryber of the New York University writes in his book 'The Conflict of religion and Science',

> "The Muslim Scientists felt that advancement is not possible through the conceptional and theoretical methods, so the way of observing the facts should be adopted in search of truth. Thus they adopted the exprimental method in their research works and relied upon the practical conclusions acquired through the senses and perceptions.
>
> "The result of this Scientific movement is evident from the great industrial developments of their age. While we read today the scientific theories in their writings it is felt as if they were the theories of our modern age. The evolution theory of the organic bodies is one of such theories which is generally understood as a modern theory but this was methodically taught in the then Muslim Schools. Their theory was much more extensive than our present one. They would apply it even upon substance and materials. [1]

They would make use of Chemistry in the Science of Medicines and in Mechanics they had advanced to the extent that they elucidated the laws of Gravity. They exposed as erroneous the Greek theory that when we look towards an object the rays of light coming out of our eyes go to that object and thus we are able to see that. On the contrary, they proved that the real position is quite reverse to this.

1. While studying such writings of the Western authors in which they try to show justice to Islam and Islamic philosophy, it is required to be very careful. The evolution theory of Darwin and Villas is quite different from that of the Muslims because the Muslims were not at war against any church or its God nor they wanted to escape from them. The Muslim scientists conceded gradual evolution on different stages. They would start their deliberations, with characteristics of the most inferior phenomena of the botanical life. According to them the gradual phases of botanical life manifest at last, in the most inferior phenomenon of animal life and thus life goes on evolving. All these happen according to the Will and intention of Allah and this is stimulating force. On the contrary, Darwin did not concede the interference of any supernatural force. He rebelled against the Church and its God, for Science and Scientific research were banned in the name of the church and its God, and those who studied science were subjected to oppressions. On the other hand, in the research works of the Muslims, there is no shadow of contempt for mankind. They did not try to condemn man as an animal without soul and cover him under the cloak of animal. In Islamic theory, it has been well explained that man has been sent to this world as a free creature. The superior position that man has over the other creatures in respect of limbs, body structure and mental and spiritual faculties, is the result of the Will of Almighty Allah, Who is the Creator of all and has fixed specific position for every creature. This shows the deep fundamental difference between the evolution theory of Darwin and Villas on one hand and that of the Muslims on the other. The Muslims, however, had presented their theory much before Europe did.

They had also the knowledge of Reflection and Reflexive light. Ibn-al-Haithem discovered that the rays of light passing through the atmosphere adopt a curved arched way. He also proved that the sun and the moon are seen before they rise on the horizon. Similarly, they are visible for a while even after they are set."

These instances are quite sufficient to explain how deeply Islam and the Islamic way of life affected mankind, its history and the great global movements. The purpose is to explain the great and multilateral truth that is often hidden from our view and because of our simplicity and ignorance, we think that we have no share in the formation of the present culture. This is free from our influences. In fact its impact is much greater than we or our history demonstrate. It is a matter of surprise that we are not even aware of our own history, and our knowledge of our own history is adopted from our enemies, whose greatest aim is to disappoint us about leading life according to the Islamic instructions and put them into practice. They get benefit from our disappointment because in this way they are saved from our counter-attacks and get rid of any anxiety from our side that we may take away the world leadership from them and keep it under our control. What a complex is that we admit their description in toto and repeat them like a parrot or monkey !

At present, however, this discussion is out of our topic, here we are to point out the marks left by the first Islamic movement that are well known to mankind. The man today is far more capable to consider and understand them than before. This capability is an addition to man's ancient nature.

CHAPTER 7

THE FOOTPRINTS ON PATH

When the first era of Islam passed and the ignorance which was ousted from power by Islam, again got hold of power; and when the Satan being ready for a new clash, once again called his followers – who till then had again captured power--then in spite of the dominane of the ignorance, the humanity could not be strayed and misled up to the extent, it had been before the advent of Islam. The cause was that, in spite of Islam being deprived of the world leadership, it remained present in the field as a force to be reckoned. Its footprints left on the path existed before the people. The principle of life it granted to the world, too were current in human life and people were well aware of them. The principles of Islam were no longer strange to the world, rather they were well known to it. The alienation which man had felt for them in the beginning of Islam, was removed now. We want to point out in this chapter those conspicuous footprints and principle of Islam.

The Unity of Mankind

Before Islam, the people of Arabia were engulfed in the slavery of tribes, castes and dynasties. These were the centre and axis of all their loyalties. The world beyond the Arabian peninsula too was captivated by the prejudices of country, homeland, colour and race. Mankind was not aware of any such superior ideal that deserved its loyalty and obedience. It was Islam, which for the first time told that the entire humanity is a single unit. Its origin is one and its goal is one Allah. It taught man that the distinctions of races, homelands and dynasties were not to divide human beings from one another and create hostility and estrangement among them, but their aim was only to identify with one another so that they might be able to recognize one another and accomplish the responsibilities that laid upon them as the viceroy of Allah on the earth; and when after death, they would return to their Lord, Who had entrusted to them the vicegerence on earch, they may be exonerated. The holy Quran, addressing man says:

> "O Mankind, Lo ! We have created you male and female, and have made you nations and tribes that you may know one another. Lo! the noblest of you, in the sight of Allah, is the best in conduct. Lo ! Allah is Knower, Aware." (AL-QURAN, 49 : 13)

> "O mankind ! fear your Lord Who created you from a single soul and from it created its mate and from them twain has spread abroad a multitude of men and women. Fear your Allah in Whom you claim (Your rights) of one another, and toward the wombs (that bore you). Lo! Allah has been a Watcher over you". (AL-QURAN, 4 : 1)

> "And of His signs is the creation of the heavens and the earth and the difference of your languages and colours. Lo ! herein indeed are portents for men of knowledge". (AL-QURAN, 30 : 22)

The principles laid down in the above-mentioned verses are not merely theoretical and conceptional, but they are practical facts of Islamic life. The authority of Islam was established in a vast and extensive part of the globe wherein inhabited people of various races and colours. Islam joined them all with the relation of one Faith and made a co-related and consolidated unity of them. It did never allow the differences of race, colour, dynasty or class to intervene this unity. These differences could not harm their brotherhood and fraternity. Nobody was ever deprived of, on the basis of these differences, any lawful rank or position which he deserved as a man.

This teaching of Islam, in the beginning, occurred as strange to the people of the world so they refused to accept it. But, eventually, this admitted fact became a part and parcel of the human conscience. Thus, despite the force of Islam being diminished after the first era, the world could neither reject it totally nor could alienate it. Its all alienation and estrangement were effaced.

It is right that mankind could not perform it as properly and good-mannerly as it was manifested in the Islamic society, and in the Muslim society too it was not practised in its complete form. This is also correct that even today the prejudices of homeland, race, nation, colour and language do exist and still there are people who are involved in such things up to the degree of insanity. It is also correct that in America and Africa the problem of the coloured race has become very dangerous and insoluble, and in Europe too it is active internally. All these are correct, but along with these things, this is also a fact that the idea of human unity has become an integral part of human intellect and its echo is heard in all the world organizations. Unity of mankind – a conception granted by Islam is the essence of modern human thinking, it is interwoven in it. All the small and limited loyalties against it are rapidly vanishing as they have neither any reasonable footing to stand nor have any status and position.

By the end of its first era, Islam had already with the help of human nature, made this idea firm in people's mind. So, for the coming generations Islam has left as its heritage not only the capital of human nature, but also has decorated it with all those means and resources that came into being through its influences. This is the reason that so far the understanding of the call of Islam and its enforcement in practical life is concerned, man of today is closer to them than the man of yesterday. His nature is more familiar to the call of Islam and now hearing it, he does not feel any alienation.

Respect for Humanity

At the time when Islam came all the respectable and honourable ranks were reserved for some particular classes and dynasties. In this world common people had no importance and any position. Islam taught the world the respect of man in a very heartfelt and effective manner. It taught that man's respect and nobility did not depend upon the random events like race, colour, class, wealth or position and rank but the real base of respect and nobility was humanity. As a man everybody was respectable and honourable. Man's genuine rights were also a demand of humanity and had the equal base.

Addressing the man, Allah says:

> "Verily We have honoured the children of Adam. We carry them on the land and the sea, and have made provision of good things for them, and have preferred them above many of those whom We created with a marked preferment." (17 : 70)

> "And when thy Lord said unto the angels: Lo ! I am about to place a viceroy in the earth, they said: Wilt Thou place terein one who will do harm therein and will shed blood, while we hymn." (2 : 30)

"And when We said unto the angels: Prostrate yourselves before Adam, they fell prostrate, all save Iblis. He demurred through pride, and so became a disbeliever." (2 : 34)

"And has made of service unto you whatsoever is in the heavens and whatsoever is in the earth, it is all from Him." (45 : 13)

From here people came to know that man is honourable before Allah being a man. This honour and status is not subject to race, colour, land, nation tribe, family, or some other casual and superficial reasons like that but it is a natural right of man. It depends, wholly, upon humanity and being an individual of the kind designated by Allah as respectable.

These are not mere theoretical conceptions but real and practical facts that have been illustrated by Islam through the formation of Muslim society. The world came to know these facts through the Muslim society. The Muslim society showed them through their practical life. And from here the common man, who had no place in society, became aware of his value and position – and conscious of his human rights. Now he came to know that even the kings and rulers were liable to accountability. From here the common people began to feel that they are free and it is below the dignity of mankind if they bear any humiliation, insult or disrespect. On the other hand the kings and rulers were made to understand that they had no such special rights which the common people were not entitled to so they should refrain from inflicting any injury to anybody's honour and prestige.

In fact, this was the new birth of man; a birth which was more important than his first physical one, for the man deprived of human honour, prestige and rights is not man in true sense of the word. If his rights are not based upon his genuine nature and temperament, which never changes or alters then where does the human prestige remain?

Hazrat Abu Bakr (R.A.A.) declared at the very beginning of his Caliphate:

> "O people! have been made your ruler, but I am not the best person among you. If I do good, help me: but If I commit mistake, put me right. Obey me as long as I obey the Commands of Allah and His Prophet (S.A.W.), but if I disobey their commands you need not obey me."

Hazrat Umer-Ibn-Al-Khattab R.A.A.) making the people aware of their rights in respect of the rulers, declared:

> "O people, I have not appointed my governors to humiliate and disrespect you and to snatch your wealth from you. I have sent them to teach you the Faith and the way of life. If anybody is maltreated then he should come and inform me. By Allah, under whose possession is Umer's life I must take revenge for him."

Hearing this Hazrat Amr-bin-'Aas stood up and asked:

> "O Chief of the faithful, in case a Muslim ruler maltreats a non-Muslim subject then would you also take revenge?"

Hazrat Umer (R.A.A.) replied:

> "By the Divine Being, under whose possession is Umer's life, I must take revenge for him also. Why should I not do that when I have seen the Messenger of Allah (S.A.W.) taking revenge even from his ownself? Do not beat the people as it is an insult to them. Do not separate them from their families and homes, as in this way they may be subjected to any mischief. Do not deprive them of their rights because they may be tended to disbelieve."

Hazrat Usman (R.A.A.) wrote to all the governors of the state:

> "I order all the governors to meet me every year on the occasion of Hajj. I have been made ruler to ordain virtures and to prohibit evils. So nobody should be subjected to any such restriction for which I have not given sanction. Neither I nor any of my governors have any (specific) rights on the nation. It is stated in Medina that a particular group of people has been humiliated and beaten, so anybody having such complaint should come to meet me on the occasion of Hajj. I shall pay back his rights lying with myself or with any of my governors. Or (if they do not want to complain) they should forgive one another. Allah likes them who forgive others."

As we have already stated, the main point in this connection is that it was not merely an expression of the theoretical principles or the utterance of hollow words, but all these were practically observed in the affaris of life in quite a realistic way and these principles flourished among the people as the practical way of life.

As an evidence to this, the instance of the copt's son may be cited who had competed in a race to the son of the conqueror and governor of Egypt, Amr-bin-Aas and had won the race. For this he was beaten by the son of Amr-bin-Aas. The copt made a complaint against this to Hazrat Umar (R.A.A.). who punished the son of Hazrat Amr-bin-Aas (R.A.A.) during the days of Hajj.

In this connection the writers generally, think it sufficient to commend the justice of Hazrat Umer (R.A.A.) only, but in fact, this event shows how Islam granted liberty to the human mind and soul. At that time Egypt was a conquered land and had recently entered the fold of Islam. The oppressed copt came from the defeated Egyptian nation and had no importance. On the other hand. Hazrat Amr-bin-Aas (R.A.A.) was the conqueror and the first governor of the country, appointed by the Islamic state. Before the Muslims, the Byzantine rulers had made the country as their colony. They were habituous of whipping the Egyptians ruthlessly. Most probably the copt too, who made complaint to Hazrat Umar (R.A.A.) might have some scratches of the Byzantine lashes on his back. It was the blessing of the Islamic liberation movement, that every copt, who had ever been the victim of the Byzantine lashes and humiliation, became a free and dignified man. The whipping and humiliation of the Byzantine period hade become the story of the past. From him emerged the man who had bcome so conscious of his selfrespect that when his son was beaten by the son of the governor, he became restelss and enraged. And in that very state he travelled from Egypt to Medina, not by a plane, car, steamship or by any other vehicle but on the back of a camel. He took the trouble of a several months long journey only to make a complaint to the Caliph who just after conquering his country had granted him the decree of freedom and made him able to recollect the lesson of human dignity and prestige that he had forgotten during the oppressive and cruel Byzantine rule.

It is correct that mankind in its history, could not ascend again to that lofty positon but the Islamic teachings left deep and undying impressions of human dignity, liberty and rights of common people in the face of the rulers and kings. These influences are still active in the present world behind the talks of 'human rights.'

It is correct that as a result of this declaration of 'human rights' nothing has come forward as a practical way of human life; undoubtedly, in the different corners of the present world man is subjected to hatred, humiliation, oppression and deprivation, and even today there are certain philosophies accorrding to which man has no better position than of the lifeless tools and appliances of a mechanic; man's liberty, self-respect and other superior human qualities have been sacrificed at the altar of increased income and production and to get hegemony over the world markets; but in spite of all these things the teachings of Islam have penetrated into the human minds and thoughts. Now these teachings are not as strange as they were in early days. So whenever the new movement of Islam comes across it, we shall, if God wishes, see that mankind is much nearer to Islam and Islamic indeology than before.

A Single Nation

At the time when Islam appeared, the human association was based upon race, land, common interest and material gains; but these inferior and limited loyalties had no concern with the real man and his nature. These were the characteristics of incidental and casual nature, that were associated to the genuine human nobility.

On this important issue, Islam asserted firmly and categorically its own standpoint. It defined in clear terms the mutual relations between man and man. It defined in clear terms the mutual relations between man and man. It stated that people can be neither associated on the basis of colour, race, native land and common economical interest, nor these things offer reasonable basis to differentiate between man and man. The foundations of these ties are Belief and man's relation with Allah. Man's relation with Allah is the basis of human nobility and according to this his behaviours towords life, both in this world and in the world after, are determined. When Allah infused His Spirit into the man, then he became man. He got honour and glory, and everything on the heavens and earth came under his disposal. This is the real foundation upon which human association emerges or eliminates, not those casual elements which have been added to the human essence.

Belief is the foundation of association, because it is the most superior feature of the human soul. In its absence, neither there can be any amity and unity nor it is possible for man to remain alive. Men should be united on this superior and noble foundation only. Unlike animals, common fodder, pasture and fence cannot be the foundation for human unity.

There are only two parties active in the world The party of Allah and the party of the Satan. The party of Allah unites under the banner of Allah and can be easily identified because of its distinct marks. On the other hand all those nations, classes, societies, races and individuals who rebel against Allah, are included in the party of Satan.

'Ummah' is the association of those people who are bounded by the common faith. This very faith is the foundation of their nationality. No *'Ummah'* can exist without faith, because in its absence nothing remains to unite its individuals. If there is no faith then only land, race, language and common material interest, separately or collectively, cannot make an Ummah.

To constitute an 'Ummah' there must be an ideology that can enliven the mind and heart. For this a conception is indispensable that can explain the universe and life and can strengthen man's relation with Allah with whose reflection he became man, superior to animals and worthy of dignity and honour.

Addressing the faithful, from the days of Hazrat Noah (A.S) up to the era of Hazrat Muhammad (S.A.W.), rather addressing all the faithful of every country, age, race, colour, tribe and clan till the Day of Ressurrection, Allah says in Holy Quran:

> "Your this *Ummah* is, in fact, the single one and I am your Lord, so worship Me." (21 : 92)

If Allah has allowed any distinction between man and man it is on the basis of Belief and ideology only. Save this, He has not given any importance to any distinction of family, race or land. Allah says:

> "Thou will not find folk who believe in Allah and the Last Day loving those who oppose Allah and His Messenger, even though they be their fathers or their sons or their brethren or their clan. As for such, He has written faith upon their hearts and has strengthened them with a Spirit from Him, and He will bring them into gardens underneath which rivers flow, wherein they will abide. Allah is well pleased with them, and they are well pleased with Him. They are Allah's party. Lo! is it not Allah's party who are the successful?" (58 : 22)

Allah has permitted homicide only in case when there is no other way out – that is in the Holy War for the cause of Allah. The Holy Quran has clearly distinguished between the aims of the faithful and those of the disbelievers, in the following words:

> "Those who believe do battle for the cause of Allah; and those who disbelieve do battle for the cause of idols. So fight the minions of the devil. Lo! the devil's strategy is ever weak." (4 : 74)

When these verses were revealed, people being surprised, exclaimed that how the basis of association could be the belief and faith only, instead of race, colour and commerce or some other likewise material basis. When Islam at first declared this 'Communalism', as it is termed in modern language, the world felt it as strange, but today we are seeing that the world is rapidly adopting this idea, and efforts are being made to unite the peoples of different countries, nations, colours and races, who speak different languages, on the basis of belief and ideology only.

It is right that in the present world the faith in God could not be the basis of human association; various groups of people are being united only on the basis of economical or social theories and the mental and ideological level of man is lower than before. The elements of secondary nature have become more attractive for man than the real and great Truth but it is also a fact, that man of today has at least admitted that belief as well as the ideological and spiritual relations and ties too can be the basis of human association. This is a vivid sign of human evolution.

Now it is up to the mankind to prepare itself for this highest and loftiest objective and step forward anew towards the greatness and loftiness, under the guidance of the coming Islamic movement. If it does so, it will find at its back all the new and old treasures of power. It will get not only the support of the human nature, but also all the weight of the experiences gained by humanity from the first Islamic movement till today, shall be on its side.

Islam taught the world to unite on the basis of faith and determined it the root of friendship and enmity. But it never considered disbelieving as the cause of enmity. It did never allow intolerance against the people who refused to accept this faith or did not agree to adopt it as the basis of their association.

Allah did not make *Jehad* (the Holy War) obligatory for the Muslims so that they should convert people forcibly to Islam. But its prupose was to enforce in the world the just, virtuous and noble system which He likes. Under this system people get full liberty to adopt any doctrine they like. By virture of its fully equitable disposition this system equally full of blessings for both the Muslims and non-Muslims.

> "There is no compulsion in religion. The right direction is henceforth distinct from error. And he who rejects false deities and believes in Allah has grasped a firm handhold which will never break. Allah is Hearer, Knower. (2 : 256)

The countries wherein Islamic order is established and Islamic Shariah is enforced, are called *"Darul Islam"* (The Land of Islam). Whether all the inhabitants therein are faithful or some of them follow other religions does not matter. In the same way the regions where no Islamic order is established, nor the Islamic Shariah is enforced are called *"Darul Harb"* (The Land at War). In this case also the religion of the people therein has nothing to do.

Islam never disregarded the mutual relations between *Darul Islam* and *Darul Harb,* rather it has fomred clear and definite principles and regulations in the light of superior moral character, Purity and virtures. So, if there exists any treaty between Darul Islam and Darul Harb it is obligatory for the *Darul Islam* to observe it fully. In this connection no treachery, deceit, one-sided abrogation of the treaty or sudden attack is permitted.

If, however, the term of the treaty ends or the people of *Darul Harb* defy it then the Muslims are allowed to declare the abrogation of the treaty and take appropriate action.

If there exists peace between the parties concerned

and there is no fixed period for that, then peace must be observed. If there is apprehension that the opposite party *(Darul Harb)* may defy it, then the agreement of peace may be abrogated, and its abrogation must be openly declared. If there happens a war, Islam has defined set principles and regulations for it also which must be observed. If the enemy tends to peace and for that purpose wants to have a regular pact to pay 'Jizya' or for the obedience of the Islamic order keeping his freedom of faith, then he may demand for it from the Muslims :

> "Lo! the worst of beasts in Allah's sight are the ungrateful who will not believe; Those of them with whom thou hadst a treaty, and they keep out duty (to Allah). if thou comest on them in the war, deal with them so as to strike fear in those who come behind them that haply they may remember. And if thou fearest treachery from any folk, then throw back to them (their treaty) fairly. Lo ! Allah loveth not the treacherous. And let not those who disbelieve suppose that they can outstrip (Allah's purpose). Lo! they cannot escape. Make ready for them all thou canst of (armed) force and of horses tethered, that thereby ye may dismay the enemy of Allah and your enemy and others beside them whom ye know not, Allah knows them. Whatsoever ye spend in the way of Allah it will be repaid to you in full, and ye will not be wronged. And if they inclined to peace, incline thou also to it, and trust in Allah. Lo! He is the Hearer, the Knower." (8 : 55 – 61)

Allah has laid stress on observing pacts and has strictly prohibited to break promises in the name of "State's interests."

> "Fulfil the convenant of Allah when you convenanted, and break not your oaths after the assertion of them, and after you have made Allah surety over you. Lo ! Allah knows what you do. And be not like unto her who unravelleth the thread, after she hath made it strong, to thin filaments, making your oaths a deceit between you because of a nation being more numerous than (another) nation. Allah only tries you thereby, and He verily will explain to you on the Day of Resurrection that wherein you differed." (16 : 91 – 92)

In case of war, nobody is allowed to be humiliated. Killing of children, old people and women is prohibited. Burning of crops and killing of cattles are not allowed; nor it is permissible to take revenge of the oppressive acts committed by the enemy. Only those are permitted to be killed who take active part in armed conflicts against the Muslims.

While bidding farewel to the Islamic army under the command of Hazrat Usama (R.A.A.), to fight against the Byzantines, Hazrat Abu Bakr (R.A.A.) issued the following guiding principles for the troops in the battlefield:

> "You shall not commit deceit, breach of trust or betrayal. You shall not avenge oppression with oppression, nor shall kill children, old men and women. You shall not cut date or any other fruit-bearing trees and shall not slaughter camels and goats but for food. You will find certain people living in solitude, leave them as they are and go to your own way with the Name of Allah."

Here I do not want to elaborate the Islamic laws regarding the relations between *Darul Islam* and *Darul Harb* or between the Muslims and non-Muslims. It is not possible to discuss such things in this article. Here I intend to describe only those general principles that Islam has formulated in regard to the mutual relations between two opposite forces. The fact is that there existed no such principles before Islam, in the world. Before Islam, the nations of the world would resort to sword for settling their issues. They would adopt the rule of non-tolerance. Everything in this world was lawful for the powerful, while the weak and defeated people had neither any right nor any refuge.

Since then till today, the principles formulated by Islam could not be excluded from human life. Not only this much, but after the Seventh century A.D. the different nations of the world consolidated their mutual relations on the basis of these very principles. From here emerged the idea of the 'International Law' and in the Nineteenth century A.D. various world organizations came into being with an effort to make it strong. Till today, the success or failure of these organizations is not of even nature, and detailed discussions are there on the 'International Law.'

In short, today the Islamic system is not estrange for the world as it was at the time of its advent. It is right, that man today has not been able to ascend up to that loftiness of character where the Muslims once had been by co opera-ting and co-ordinating with the other nations of the world. This is also correct, that during the current century the theories of International Law, formulated by the Western philosophy of life had to suffer a serious setback and the principles of the declaration of war and abrogation of pacts in the syste matic way have been abolished. Today massacre, devastation and destruction are more prevelent among the human beings than the wild beasts. This is also correct wheter it is war or peace, the main objects of the contending powers remain materialistic hegemony, plundering wealth and seeking new markets for their products which cannot be compared to the lofty object and high values of belief, faith, virtues and justice of the Islamic Jehad. But despite all these things this fact remains intact that the conception of International relations under the law approved by nations concerned, was introduced to the world by Islam. And it is this order of virtue and greatness formulated by Allah for mankind that translated this idea into practice.

If man is again called to this straight Path, it will not be a new one for him, nor he will feel any confusion in this. Being unaware of the Divine Guidance and going astray in the darkness of ignorance, man may be apathetic towards the glorious moral foundation of Islam, but so far the ideology is concerned, it is neither new for him nor he will feel any confusion in recognizing it. At its advent, Islam had the only capital of human nature to elucidate and consolidate its principles. But in future, if an Islamic movement starts; it will get full advantage of the intimacy and consciousness that already exists in mankind about some of its principles. As also the experience gained by man in the meantime shall also be advantageous for it. And thus, if God wishes, the movement will march forward with better abilities and force towards its goal.

CHAPTER 8

THE LAST WORD

There is not much space in this brief article as to environ all the marks and effects left by Islam on the human history and on the present human life. Time has made these marks and effects dim and has mutilated them a lot. There is also a great distance between them and the loftiness where man was made to ascend by this revealed path of virtue and greatness. But in spite of this, it is a fact that those marks and effects could never cease to exist – and before Islam these marks and effects are not found anywhere else.

Through the few instances we have cited in this book the countless effects left by Islam on the world history can be evaluated. The history of the last fourteen hundred years is full of such examples.

In the conclusion of these discussions, we want to warn the preachers of Islam that while seeing the favourable conditions and components, they should not be misled by any wishful thinking and should never overlook the difficulties and obstructions on the path. At this juncture, we want to say that they should also keep an eye over the difficulties of the path.

Today man is much more far off Allah than before. The curtains of ignorance today on human nature are more thick and dark than before. The ancient ignorance was the product of man's general ignorance, simplicity and the age of wildness. On the contrary, the modern ignorance is the result of his knowledge, perplexity and superficiality.

The man of the eighteenth and nineteenth centuries was stunned by the conquests of science. In the name of church and its God, the enlightened and learned people were burnt alive and were subjected to oppressions and violence. This excited such a violent indignation among the people that no sacred thing was spared.

This is right, that with the commencement of the current century, science once again is attentive to God and the great scientists, by dint of their studies, are being convinced of the Divine Being; it seems that mankind being tired of going astray in the desert of disbelief and infidelity, is again returning to its Lord, but many eyes are still dazzled owing to the materialistic splendours of science. On account of this, the strayed caravan of mankind may come probably, to its senses at the end of the current century and will come thoroughly out of the desolation of disbelief.

Man of today is much more temporal in his feelings, emotions and life. The circle of his temporal life and scope of his influences too are more extensive than before. As a result of the luxuries, ease and comforts provided by the modern culture, the human life is materially very vast. The modern man is well aware of the vastness and importance of the temporal life. Science, culture and arts have apprised human life, emotions and feelings of many new worlds.

Had there been, behind these phenomena; active the devotion to Allah and man would have been aware of the Qualities of Allah and he had the true sense of the relation between Allah and himself – in other words, if the materialistic developments would have been based upon the fact that man is the viceroy of Allah on the earth, Who has equipped him with all the necessary qualities and qualifications, required to utilize all the things on earth, so that he may be tested in this world that how far he deserves the perpetual pleasures of the next world; if there had been progress on this basis, then the present developments of science and culture would imply the developments of faith and religion. The new conquests of man would have caused the extension of his religious sense and consciousness and man would have been much nearer than before, to Allah and His path of virture i.e. Islam.

But as we know, the present progress is the outcome of the rebellion against a tyrannical church and its God in whose name man was subjected to oppressions and violence; so the present progress, instead of bringing man nearer to Allah, has turned against Him and has become the cause of taking man away from Him. It stands as an obstruction between the Right path and the man. The promoters of Islam, while preaching for it, should always keep in view this fact.

Actually, the man of today is disgusted at the distructions caused by the materialistic culture and the plenty of luxuries. As a matter of fact, vices and corruptions as also the nervous and mental diseases and sensual disorders are devouring the Western culture like weevils and nations as well as individuals are being doomed. Thus people's eyes are being opened and they have started to perceive the wrongs and vices.

But in spite of this, beastliness prevails over man of today, an insanely unconsciousness has got hold of him. His life is subjected to confusion and turmoil. It seems that man cannot come to his senses before the current century ends. This much time is indispensable for getting rid of his mental unconsciousness and to do away with the dazzling of his eyes.

The primeval ignorance was connected to the nomadic life of wild age which had vivid influence over it. The character of the people in those days was, up to a large extent, under the control of the nomadic traditions of life. This caused a vigorous conflict between the call of Islam and the ignorance. But there was no confusion or anything complex everything was vivid and clear. The path of the faith was clear and the infidelity too was explained. That is why despite the thick covers of obstinacy, stubbornness, pride and haughtiness, the reaction of the human nature too was quite clear. Evidently, this situation was far better than the present state of coldness, superficiality, sensuality and ideological instability.

So far beliefs, theories and philosophy of life are concened, man of today is quite shallow and cold. Rather he is, not serious at all in these matters. His life is full of hypocrisy, deception, fruad and meanness. These are the various obstructions on the way of calling man to the faith of Allah and to lead him towards this path. These obstructions do not allow man to progress towards Allah.

The preachers of Islam should keep in view all these things so that seeing the favourable circumstances and aspects, they should not become the victim of misunderstanding and be sluggish towards their due preparations. They should not think these obstructions as trivial nor should ignore them.

Now, what is the proper method of carrying the message of Islam? Those who serve Islam should take care of one thing in this regard that is piety! This is the only baggage in this journey. Its true sense is that man should always keep in mind Allah with all His Qualities and Attributes – He should feel that whatever he is doing, is doing with the direct help of Allah. He should have unshaken faith in this promise of Allah.

"To help believers is incumbent upon Us." (30 : 47)

The only demand of Islam from the believers is that they should have full reliance on Allah and should go forward by means of that. They should consider the promise of Allah as the greatest reality of the world. To gain the Pleasure of

Allah, should be the aim and object of their life and of all struggles. It is the party of the faithfuls through which the law of Allah in regard to the establishment of His faith comes to light. Through this party the human nature gets rid of the rubbish of ignorance. And thus the command of Allah that His Will must prevail on the earth and power should remain under the control of His faith, is accomplished.

> Systems have passed away before you. Do but travel in the land and see the nation of the consequence for those who did deny (the Messenger). This is a declaration for mankind, a guidance and an admonition unto those who ward off (evil). Faint not nor grieve, for you will overcome them if you are (indeed) believers. If you have received a blow, the disbelieving people have received a blow the like thereof. These are (only) rhe vicissitudes which we cause to follow one another for mankind, to the end that Allah may know those who believe and may choose martyrs from among you; and Allah loves not wrongdoers. And that Allah may prove those who believe, and may blight the disbelievers."
>
> (3 : 137 - 141)

THE END